Sowing the Seeds of Love

In memory of
Joseph Michael Leith

JOSEPHINE FEENEY

Sowing the Seeds of Love

A LION BOOK

Copyright © 1999 Josephine Feeney

The author asserts the moral right
to be identified as the author of this work

Published by
Lion Publishing plc
Sandy Lane West, Oxford, England
www.lion-publishing.co.uk
ISBN 0 7459 3911 2

First edition 1999
10 9 8 7 6 5 4 3 2 1 0

A catalogue record for this book is available
from the British Library

Typeset in 13/16 Caslon Old Face
Printed and bound in Great Britain by
Caledonian International Book Manufacturing, Glasgow

Contents

A Power so Divine   9

A Few Words About This Book   11

Part One: Home and Hearth
*How Faith and Spirituality Affect the Way We Nurture
Our Children*

One: Before Birth   19

Two: The Early Days – Heaven Is Like This, Really?   27

Three: Watching the Moon and Stars – Coping With
Broken Nights   34

Four: The Shock of the Tantrum   40

Five: I Was Sick and You Visited Me   48

Six: Refusing to Feast   55

Seven: Training the Unmentionable   62

Eight: Play With Me, Play With Me – A Spiritual
    Approach to Toys   67

Nine: Going to Church   74

Part Two: Church and Chapel
How Churches Welcome Children

One: Whatever Has Happened to Our Sabbath?   83

Two: What Is the Point of Going to Church on
    Sunday?   89

Three: Suffer Little Children… to Come to Our
    Church   96

Four: Welcoming   100

Five: Provision for the Child   109

Six: Liturgy and Worship   118

Seven: Bible Teaching   125

Eight: Support for Parents   132

Nine: Churches and Children   138

Ten: The Big Question   144

Eleven: Celebrate!   150

Acknowledgments   157

Bibliography   159

A Power So Divine

It's three o'clock in the morning, again. New Year's Day. I have slept for an hour and a half and the cries emerge from the baby's room with great urgency.

My head is heavy with the New Year toast and the desperate need for sleep. I lift the baby out, creep from the room and, lying in bed, I feed her. For a few precious moments there is idyllic peace as we comfort one another. I close my eyes and begin to drift off, almost dreaming, then the baby wriggles and struggles. She's uncomfortable – nappy needs changing. In the cold, dark room I fumble with pins and plastic pants then I lie back and cuddle her again, longing for sleep. She protests – teething? I search for a comforting balm to settle her but still she writhes about uncomfortably.

I put her over my shoulder, pat her back, we wander about the room. I talk to her, tell her about the day she was born – how I made pastry in the early morning and placed it in the fridge ready to be rolled out later in the day. 'The pie was never made,' I say. She laughs, chortles, but still she won't sleep.

I sit on the bed, wide awake now but longing to return to the warmth and comfort of sleep. I hum, searching my aching head for words. A song creeps out of my memory, a song once sung to me with love and tenderness. 'You're my world, you are my night and day,' I sing. 'You are my world, you are my night and day, child,' I whisper, reiterating the lyrics. With a croaky voice I quietly aim to reach the right note.

> You're my world, you're every breath I take.
> You're my world, you're every move I make.
> Other eyes see the stars up in the sky,
> But for me, they shine within your eyes.
> As the trees reach for the sun above,
> So my arms reach out to you, for love.
> With your hand, resting in mine,
> I feel a power so divine…

The phrase warms me and hits me like a winter toddy. I whisper, 'You, child, are a power so divine.'

In the bleak hours of a winter's night, the miracle of our child's existence is revealed to me again. I am excited with my new discovery. I want to hug and cuddle and tickle her but she's asleep. I place her carefully in the cot and stroke her velvety face.

'You're my world,' I say. 'You're a power so divine.'

A Few Words About This Book

At the local Pram Club we talk about everything – feeding, sleeping, teething, nappies, walking, weaning and clothing. We compare cots, prams, buggies, playpens, high chairs, potties, stair gates, alarms, car seats and swings. We share details about meal times, nap times, bed times and play times. We listen to tales of broken nights, temper tantrums, accidents and illnesses. Occasionally, very occasionally, we reveal a little about our social life. However, in four years of talking in great detail about my children, I have rarely spoken about, or heard another person speak about, the child's spiritual life.

Nobody has sat next to me at the Pram Club, cup of coffee and biscuit in hand, and said, 'How do you pray with your baby?' I have never discussed the spiritual welfare of my children with anyone outside of our home and I suspect that is the case for many parents.

We talk about everything at our Pram Club – well, almost everything. We forget to mention a vitally important aspect of our child's development and, strangely, most Pram Clubs and Mums and Toddlers groups meet on church premises. In my own area, the Baptist Church holds one on Monday; the Elim Pentecostal on a Tuesday; the Congregational on a Wednesday; Anglican on a Thursday and Methodist on Friday. The hospitality is excellent and the good people of these communities provide a vital service for parents and toddlers. But God rarely gets a mention.

Why am I so hesitant, so reluctant to talk about praying with my baby, my 'power so divine'? What is it about faith and spirituality that we consider too personal to share with others? Why are we so quiet, so reserved when it comes to the faith and the spirituality of our children?

Over the last few years the numbers of people attending church services in some countries, including Britain, have dropped considerably for all sorts of reasons. Many young people have distanced themselves from the organized church and think that organized religion is no longer necessary. Yet, in early Autumn 1997, the death of Diana, Princess of Wales, showed that the UK was not a spiritually empty country. Even the Archbishop of Canterbury noted the sentiments expressed on bouquets and messages of condolence: 'God bless you, Diana. May you rest in peace.' 'We are sure you're in heaven.' Britain mourned and as one, it seemed, watched a religious service tailored to the mood of the day. So, although Britons may not be packing the pews, they're certainly not a country of heathens, either.

Many parents genuinely want a spiritual life, a faith, for their children but they may ask, 'Where do I start?' If they have, long ago, distanced themselves from the organized church, it's hard to know how to find a way back in. That's what this book is about: sowing the seed, developing and nurturing faith and spirituality in babies and toddlers. But it isn't just about telling people to return to church. Parenting with a spiritual focus demands much more than a weekly visit to church. Our faith affects every part of our being – every action, every thought and every word. Otherwise our faith is a hollow one. So in this book I'll also present a personal, Christian approach to parenting, one which can bring great rewards.

I write this book as a Christian for Christians and for those of other faiths who wish to develop a spirituality in their very young children. You may be a practising Christian or someone who was brought up as a Christian but has long ago ceased any organized practice of the faith. Or you may have your own form of spirituality. Now you're looking for something extra for your child, something far more important than the luxury prams and cots we are seduced into buying.

No apologies are made for writing this from a Christian perspective – I can only write as I am! Which leads me to another point, perhaps you could call it a confession. I'm not a theologian or a scripture scholar – I'm a mother and a writer. My parents were not scripture scholars, either, but they encouraged and nurtured a living faith; a way of life that has been passed down from parent to child for the last 2,000 years, since the birth, death and resurrection of Jesus Christ. So, I write as a Christian and a mother.

My experience as a mother, great though I may consider it to be, is very limited. I have two wonderful children who have, along with their father, transformed my life. However, I could not consider myself to be either a perfect parent or an expert on mothercare. That's why I asked others for their thoughts and opinions on parenting.

As if in answer to a prayer, a friend invited me to be part of a parenting course. All the sessions helped us as families to cope with the stresses of everyday life with pre-school children. The course also provided me with a ready-made group of people who were also striving to be good parents or, in the words of the handbook, 'good-enough parents'. Most but not all of the participants were Christians.

I have been deeply affected by this parenting course and also by the friendship and support I received from others on the course. So, along with my thoughts and suggestions, I also include those of my fellow participants. Just reading them was an inspiring and humbling experience for me – especially when I considered that these were people I had known for several years through our local Pram Club, where we had never before talked about our children's faith or about how our own faith affected the way we raised our children.

In the first part of this book I will look at how faith is nurtured at home and how a life of faith affects the ways in which we cope with different stages of a child's development. Then, I'll look at the organized church to see how babies are welcomed and cared for, how the church responds to the words of Jesus: 'Suffer little children to come unto me, for theirs is the kingdom of heaven.' My research in this area has been limited to the western part of my home town but it will mirror the facilities available in other urban and rural communities throughout Britain and perhaps elsewhere.

This book doesn't have all the answers about faith. I'm still learning how to nurture a faith in my children. Quite often on Sundays, after an hour of wrestling with the squirming of two children at church, my husband and I ask ourselves, 'What are we doing here?' It's hard to listen to God's word or to gain any inspiration when we're so preoccupied with things like behaviour. Maybe this is part of the reason we don't discuss our children's spiritual development at Mums and Toddlers groups.

Whatever the circumstances of our children's births, they are a vibrant, real and precious presence in our lives.

We can treasure them as a 'power so divine' as well as developing in them a sense of the divine, a sense of the sacred. I hope this book will help and encourage you in the first stage of your child's life. For that is what we all need: love, help, hope and encouragement – not to mention a good night's sleep.

Part One

Home and Hearth

How Faith and Spirituality Affect the Way We Nurture Our Children

One

Before Birth

'Before I formed you in the womb,
I knew you...'
Jeremiah 1:5

The word of God to the prophet Jeremiah in the Bible reinforces the presence of the divine in the unborn child, from the very second of creation. But in a society ambiguous about pregnancy, it's very hard to be positive when a mother discovers her pregnancy test is positive.

When I thought I was pregnant with my first baby, I dutifully went to the clinic with my sample. On arriving there, the nurse took my sample, disappeared for ages and then on her return asked, 'Is this good news?'

'What do you mean?' I asked. 'What's the result?'

'Oh... sorry,' she said, apologetically. 'It's positive. Is it good news?'

'I don't understand you,' I said.

'Is it planned, expected? Are you in a stable relationship?'

There, right at the very beginning of life, a miracle goes unacknowledged. The sacredness of that precious moment is marred by an unnecessary question.

Why do we have to qualify miracles? Perhaps our lives are so carefully planned, so precisely divided into years and days and minutes, that there's no room for the miraculous, no room for the divine. Acknowledging miracles and divinity means letting go and thinking of a little more than the latest style in buggies.

The nurse's question did little to stem our joy. But the elation didn't last long once the sickness started. Through the sickness and fatigue it really is hard to feel that something wonderful is happening. First pregnancy is like a constant state of unknowing – longing to know what's going to happen next but dreading to experience it. There's a sense in which you're looking forward, with great hope and optimism, to the birth of your child but also filled with worry about how you'll cope with actually being a parent. Thinking about the spiritual development of your baby is probably a long way down your list of concerns, but thinking of your child as a person in his or her own right helps in the way you care for yourself during pregnancy and in preparing for labour and birth.

When I was pregnant with my first child, I wrote him a letter while stuck in a traffic queue:

Dear child,

We're in a traffic jam – a five-mile tail-back and then a further five miles of road works. Work commenced in March for ten weeks. When it's over, you'll be born. Our life is measured in weeks – seven more weeks, thirty-three weeks gone.

An American voice speaks from the car radio about the excitement of fibre optics. 'One strand will be able to take the whole of the United States' messages for Mother's Day.'

'But can they cure heartburn?' I ask your father, 'Or backache?' The most sophisticated technology cannot match you, my child, or the discomfort you cause.

You have changed my life, child. Never before did I imagine that so much could grow and develop during ten weeks of traffic queues – you have gained weight and lengthened, your kicks have strengthened, and the heartburn... the heartburn dominates the latter part of each day.

We are lucky, child, for many women have to face the sickness, the tiredness, the pains, the heartburn and the heartache all alone. You kick and I remember, once again, how precious and fragile you are. You have taught me so much, child. If I were alone and faced with a future of poverty and hardship, I might have chosen a different route.

The heartburn becomes worse. Your growing forces my stomach into a small corner. Your father passes me a peppermint, to relieve the discomfort, as we closely inspect the half-way stage of the ten-week roadworks. An accident slows the traffic further. I place my hands over my abdomen as if to shield your eyes.

Because of you, child, I have experienced great compassion and kindness and that has changed my life. What do we want for you? What do we hope for you? We want you to grow in a Christian Community; we want you to belong to a people who welcome and support single parents and families who are distressed by poverty and hardship. Most of all, if we're honest, we want you to be healthy and happy.'

We had many hopes and dreams for our first child and that pregnancy, despite the discomfort and difficulties, was a golden time in our lives.

It's important to be positive and hopeful about your unborn child's future. As well as buying the nappies, cot, pram and high chair, alongside thinking about names, it's good to actually write down your hopes for your child – not just for her future but also for the future of the community in which she'll grow. We don't exist in a vacuum or a bubble. Our child's happiness and well-being depends, to a certain extent, upon the health of the community.

Before that, there's labour and birth to manage and there are no end of people willing to tell you all about that experience. Women who have had babies (and some men who have been involved birth partners) love sharing their experiences of labour and childbirth – mostly with newly pregnant women.

Five months pregnant with my first child, I sat in a crowded staff common room, talking at first about names. 'Any ideas?' my colleagues asked. Talking about names involves everyone, it's a general subject and people love to speculate about what they might call their child. It's an innocuous and fun activity but quite often, it's just a warm-up for the really gory subject of labour.

I didn't want to hear other people's experiences of labour. At home, I shut my ears when my sisters told me how dreadful it could be and yet, here, in a crowded room I could sense the conversation hurtling towards stories of pain endured over many hours. The ending was always happy but the penultimate chapter was a Himalayan challenge.

'My labour lasted for three days,' one woman said. Her baby was nearly twenty and now away at university. 'Three days! I'll never forget it.'

'Oh, you shouldn't tell her this,' an older colleague said. 'You'll frighten her.'

'How do you cope?' I asked, trying to steer the talk away from the gory details. 'How did you cope with labour?'

'Epidural!' said one.

'I prayed… we prayed,' said the woman whose labour had lasted for days.

She spoke unselfconsciously. 'Before I went to the hospital my mum said to me, "Don't forget your prayers", and every time I felt a pain I called out in prayer. I thought of Mary in a back stable, lying on a hard floor. No midwife, no mattress, no gas and air – I asked her to think of me. Then I squeezed my husband's hand.'

'Did it work?' I asked.

'Oh yes,' came the confident reply.

Prayer in pregnancy and labour. In a secular environment, a woman spoke out about her prayer during labour. She inspired me with her deep faith and courage, caring little about what others thought of her.

I never forgot her and during a long and very difficult labour I prayed with my husband. I was also aware of many close relatives and friends praying for me – most especially, my mother, who remained awake during the long night of my labour. After thirteen hours, our child was born – healthy and well.

In an otherwise excellent antenatal service, it was interesting to note that nobody had mentioned the spiritual side of pregnancy. Many different forms of pain relief were offered to us in our antenatal group – some of these are coping strategies, rather than relief. Yet in a group which included Hindus, Moslems, Sikhs, Jews and Christians, prayer as a means of coping with the difficult moments was never mentioned.

When I asked other mothers if they had used prayer as a means of coping during labour, I received some amazing responses:

———

'When I went into labour, I committed myself into the Lord's hands and trusted him to give me success.'

Sarah, mother of two girls aged eight months and two years

———

'Through believing that God had created the child I was carrying, had designed the method of pregnancy and childbirth and would watch over us and be present at the baby's birth gave me confidence that I could trust in him and call on his help in moments of anxiety, fear and pain.'

Carmel, mother of two children aged three and six years

———

'A small network of friends began to pray for me the moment I was taken into hospital. With the problem that had cropped up in a previous pregnancy, this was a great strength.'

Kate, mother of three boys aged two, four and six years

Reflecting on my own experience of labour and birth, I was unaware, until later, of the number of people who were praying for me. It wasn't just my family and friends but people in other countries and some religious groups who pray especially during the night for mothers in labour. Even before a child is born they are welcomed with prayer by the Christian community. What a great start for a child!

Two

The Early Days: Heaven Is Like This – Really?

I once heard a sermon about heaven. 'Heaven is like the rush of joy a mother feels after the birth of her child,' the preacher said. Really? When I go to heaven, will I feel bruised and exhausted for the first few weeks? Will I burst into tears at the slightest thing God says to me and fret at every feed time?

'We don't know what heaven is like in the same way that neither a mother nor her child can even begin to contemplate how they will feel after the birth,' the preacher continued. Will I have a terrible headache, like the one our baby had for days after a forceps delivery?

I didn't feel heavenly or wonderful after our first baby was born. Nothing had prepared me for how I would feel and for many women who suffer postnatal illness, the first few months of their baby's life can be the most difficult of their own. Yes, the arrival of a new baby is a time of great joy but it can be a painful time, too.

New parents are therefore greatly supported and sustained by good wishes, prayers, cards and gifts from family and friends. Once the prayers are answered and the baby arrives, the expressions of relief and joy are immediately despatched. I will never forget the overwhelming sense of love I felt, despite the pain and worry, when the postman brought new surprises every day.

The first time we went to church with our new baby, we were surrounded and embraced with words of congratulations and kindness. The new member of our community was given such a great welcome. That part of being a new parent was heavenly and it was unexpected. I knew that we, as parents, would be thrilled. I hadn't expected other people to feel such excitement at our little bundle of the divine.

Back home, I wasn't prepared for the exhaustion and loneliness of looking after our child. I placed prayer cards in his pram and I read the prayer cards over and over, chanted them like a mantra, searching for strength and protection for our baby.

Our baby's prayer life was, therefore, very far from my mind in those early, difficult days. That is, until a good friend advised, 'Don't forget to pray with your baby.' Pray?

With my baby? It was hard to pray myself let alone think about another soul to care for, and I know that is the experience of many, many parents.

———

'I'm sad to say with hindsight, I would pray for them but not with them until later.'

Kate

———

'I did pray for both babies and asked God for strength to get us through the early months of adjustment.'

Jackie

But if we are to develop a sense of the sacred, a sense of the divine in our children we need to pray with them as they grow.

In those early weeks and months of life a child is totally dependent on parents and other carers. A young baby cannot feed himself so he's fed by his parents. The child cannot move so he's transported or carried in a variety of ways. Little by little he learns how to feed himself and how to move about. He is weaned from liquids to solids and he's supported as he starts to roll, crawl, walk and run.

Praying is like eating or moving. It's a gradual process and it's best to begin soon after birth – even if you're feeling far from heavenly. You pray with your child – or for your child. Whisper a simple prayer into his ear in the morning and evening. Say something very simple like, 'Look after me, Lord.' Perhaps make a sign of the cross on your child's forehead each time you put him down to sleep.

Let your child see you pray – example is the greatest teacher. If praying is a natural and normal part of your day then it will become the same for your child. 'Train up a child in the way he should go and when he is old, he will not depart from it.' (Proverbs 22:6)

For those who look to God, praying is as vital for good growth as eating. We can't explain to a child the nutritional importance of a good, balanced diet. So it is with prayer – we can't explain the theology behind the words we whisper into our child's ear – it would be meaningless and unnecessary to the child. The new baby needs love, warmth, food, stimulation, peace and to know he is cared for. Praying with your child is one way of showing God's care for him.

———

'We pray with both our children on a daily basis. We learn scriptures together and we read the Bible.'
Sarah

———

'We prayed for our children rather than with them as babies and as soon as they could talk we prayed with them.'
Carmel

'As my faith has grown I was far more aware of the enormous task of giving a child a taste of the things of God when they are little...'

Amanda, mother of two boys aged eighteen months and five years

Making prayer part of the normal routine of life helps children to accept it as a perfectly natural part of the day. In our home, we pray each morning – before we go our separate ways, we pray. We pray at mealtimes, bedtime and at moments of great stress and at times when we want to thank God.

I have found my children's developing spiritual awareness one of the most delightful and uplifting experiences of their childhood. Through their growing faith I have learned so much and I have had many broad smiles as they struggle with some aspects of faith.

In the mornings there's always a bit of a tussle between the two children to see who can get the best prayer book so that they can lead the prayer. But the main thing is that this is perfectly normal for them. Quite often, they remind us about the prayer.

Until recently, we said a simple grace before each meal and we tried to encourage the children to wait until grace was said before they started eating. Since the oldest child started school, this routine has changed. It's amazing to see the authority with which our child speaks when he tells us, 'Stand beside your chairs and face the crucifix.' Then, in the sing-song tone of the infant school dining room, we say the grace – just as Mrs McLoughlin, the dinner lady, leads it.

In the same way, the morning and evening prayers of school have been transported to our home – even the voice of the teacher: 'Say after me... God our Father...' And we do, we say after him and he is delighted that he is able to teach us a little of the wonderful things he learns at school.

If you are searching for a way of prayer for your children, keep it simple and short. Be sincere and honest. Children are the first to notice when words and deeds do not come from the heart. Show that God is needed in the difficult times as well as the joyful moments of celebration. Sometimes, on significant days, we light the children's baptismal candle and they watch with awe as the flame burns and illumines their prayer time. It's good to add another dimension to prayer.

When I'm tired and feeling ill, there's a dinner to be cooked and I don't feel like doing anything, I sit with my children and we pray: 'God, give me strength, help me through this day especially as I'm tired...' Then my children see my vulnerability – they comfort me and give me strength and I begin to see God's presence in our home and, therefore, an answer to my prayer.

We're not perfect by any means but we're struggling, trying hard to have a home filled with faith.

———

'Faith-filled families acknowledge Christ's presence in their midst and find rituals to celebrate this in their gatherings. This will help them remember the promise, "Where two or three are gathered in my name I am there in their midst."'

'House-based religion', by Michael H. Crosby OFM, in *Priests and People*, 2 February 1997, Tablet Publishing Company

He's also present in the daily and nightly struggles of family life and that's good for all parents to know. Especially at night!

Three

Watching the Moon and Stars – Coping With Broken Nights

It was a great shock to discover, very quickly, that our baby would need feeding in the night. Even though it was midsummer and quite light by four o'clock in the morning, I couldn't help but feel lonely and slightly cheated because everyone else was asleep and I wasn't.

One night, I fed the baby and, thinking everybody else in the world was asleep, I drew back the curtains to watch a silent world. Across the road a policeman pounded a lonely beat and a light burned in a neighbour's window. There were others in the world who were awake.

Of course others are awake. Some of those who are called to a life of prayer spend their nights praying for those who may find the darkness lonely: nursing mothers and new fathers who pace up and down to relieve wind, colic and a thousand other ailments; the homeless; carers of those who are seriously ill; members of the emergency services; broadcasters; journalists; night shift workers and those who simply can't sleep. For me, it was comforting to realize that others were awake.

That night and other nights when I fed the baby, I prayed with him. They were simple prayers, remembering all those whose lives were full of broken nights. As I rubbed his back I said, 'Look after those people who have no homes, whose nights are broken by dampness and cold. Once, as babies, they were fed and comforted. Let them be loved again.'

The lack of sleep was hard but it was a great comfort for me to know that someone, somewhere in the world was praying for me, for our baby and for other nursing mothers.

———

'It is sometimes difficult to leave a warm bed in the middle of the night… We get hundreds of prayer requests from all over the world. More than ever, there is a real need for prayer. Twenty-four hours a day we bring the pains and disasters and hurts of the world before God…'

Mother Simeon of Tyburn Convent, London, speaking to Barbara Bruce in the *Sunday Post Magazine*, 5 October 1997

'He came back and he found them sleeping and he said to Peter, "Simon, are you asleep? Had you not the strength to keep awake one hour? You should be awake and praying not to be put to the test."'

Mark 14:37–38

While we were growing up and saying the rosary each evening we giggled at the mention of the 'Agony in the Garden'. For us, it was having to do something we didn't like doing on one of Dad's two allotments. That was our personal 'Agony in the Garden'. Now I see it differently. I know what it is to be awake in the night with a crying child. I think I know how Jesus might have felt as he listened to the contented snoring of his friends.

When we brought home our first-born, it was midsummer and the nights were short. I found the feeding difficult at one o'clock in the morning but at four o'clock I felt privileged to hear the dawn chorus and see the far-away sun burst through the cloud of darkness. Despite being tired, I enjoyed that feed.

Then the nights lengthened and the days shortened. If I'd had a textbook child he should have been sleeping through the night by the middle of October, but he wasn't, and as the nights grew darker and colder, he woke in just the same way as he always did.

Our second child was another midsummer baby, a

pleasure to feed and comfort while the nights were short and the sun burst through during the dawn feed. By November, the dreadful broken nights were dragging me down. In January I felt almost broken by my inability to have one complete night's sleep. Eighteen months later I can say, quite confidently, that I have had about four unbroken nights' sleep in two and a half years. Now it has become the norm to be woken in the night. I can almost cope with it.

How do others cope with broken nights? As I read through the responses to my question, I felt both humbled and ashamed at my lack of faith and strength when I was feeding through the night. Their words, however, will bring great comfort and encouragement to those who still endure being awake at three o'clock in the morning.

———

'Wanting to give my children the best I breastfed both of them during the first year of their lives and so with that commitment, I sacrificed my nights with pleasure.'

Sarah

———

'How did I cope? Much breast feeding for comfort and I didn't attempt to do much in the day – just a lot of cuddling.'

Carmel

'I prayed – simply love of each child and asking myself, "How would Jesus deal with this child?"'

Margaret

———

'I found the broken nights very difficult. Before my baby was born I prayed that she would have a "bit of spark". I got what I asked for and this sometimes consoled me.'

Clare, mother of one daughter aged five years

———

'I enjoyed the quiet sort of intimacy with the baby while the rest of the household slept.'

Tracy, mother of four children

———

'I enjoyed feeding my second child, a summer baby, in the early hours as the house was peaceful and I could pray.'

Amanda

Mother Simeon was so right when she said, 'Nobody likes to leave a warm bed in the middle of the night.' Many parents, for the sake of their babies, will spend hours feeding, cuddling and consoling in the darkest times of the night. They are living sermons as they speak of the joy and peace they experience bringing comfort to their children.

'... *in so far as you did this to one the least of these brothers of mine, you did it for me.*'

Matthew 25:40

The sacrifices those parents make, on behalf of their children, will reap great rewards in years to come. Before that, things may not progress quite so smoothly.

Four

The Shock of
the Tantrum

It was December. The late afternoon sun painted each feature of the back room with a reddish glow belying the chill of the wintry weather outside. Trees and hedges grew darker as the sun set so early in the day. In the far distance I watched a flock of geese flying boldly across the sky, silhouetted by the darkening day. I felt peaceful and relieved that I was inside, protected from the harsh elements of the approaching evening.

I remember that day so well. I can even picture the exact position of the furniture in the room and the activity we were doing quietly, side by side, in perfect harmony. Oh yes, I remember it so well for that was the day of the very first tantrum. Other parents tell me that their memories of the first tantrum were just as vivid. 'We were in the supermarket,' or 'I was crossing a very busy road during the rush hour and there were hundreds of pairs of eyes trained on me,' or 'It was at a wedding...'

For us, it was a quiet, cosy sort of day. We'd been at Mums and Toddlers group in the morning, returning home for lunch and a nap. I was almost three months pregnant with the second child and oh – so sick. But our lives hummed along, pleasantly and gently, with very little to upset or disturb us.

In the morning he had been a delightful child, as ever, smiling most of the time or frowning if he needed a drink or his nappy changing. They were the two main emotions – happiness at almost everything or sadness when he was hungry, tired, thirsty or uncomfortable. There was no in-between and life was, apart from the sickness, smooth and easy going.

When I talked about my wonderful son – how he never brought me a moment's grief and how he was always smiling – to mothers of older children, they said, 'Wait until he hits the Terrible Twos!' I always smiled at their words for I felt it would never happen to me. I thought, with such a delightful, agreeable, perfect child, there was no way that he would have the Terrible Twos. Not my lovely, placid boy who had never witnessed anger or resentment. No, not my boy.

That's why it came as such a shock, on that winter's afternoon when he was just seventeen months old, that he should have his first tantrum. My lovely boy who had always been so good had turned, in a moment, into a kind of monster who threw himself around the room, arched his back and shrieked with truly blood-curdling screams.

Since that day there have been many more. Some time I'll tell him about the day he picked up a bottle of white spirit from Sainsbury's Homebase and demanded we buy it for him. (It was displayed in a place where supermarkets used to stack sweets and chewing gum.) I tried to explain that he didn't need it, neither did we and it would be dangerous to allow him to play with such a thing. But explanations are superfluous and unnecessary in such a situation. He was carried, kicking and screaming, from the shop by Daddy while Mummy struggled with a very young baby and ten rolls of wallpaper.

Before the tantrums started, I used to look at the parents of children who were having tantrums and think to myself, 'Why can't that parent control that child?' I was often both disgusted and amazed at the way adults managed these situations. I stared and stared, fascinated by the seeming ineptness of an adult to control a small child. Now that I've been on the receiving end of many such stares I am ashamed of how I once judged such complex situations.

It's so hard, in the midst of many conflicting emotions, for a toddler to behave rationally. When I'm hungry or tired or upset, I find it hard to be rational, be polite, be warm. How much harder must it be for a child who doesn't understand what he's feeling.

Parents work out their own way of coping with tantrums and other irrational behaviour, but every approach needs to involve patience and firmness. A parenting course I recently attended advised that parents ensure that they help their toddlers to cope with difficult emotions and control their tantrums.

————

'It's better to face up to and grow out of tantrums at three rather than at forty-three.'

Michael and Terri Quinn, *From Pram to Primary School*

In the early days I was acutely embarrassed about the public nature of my child's tantrums. My main concern was to remove him to a less prominent place or even, to meet the wishes of the reproachful stares, to address him with threats made in an aggressive tone. 'If you don't stand up this minute then I'll…'

Then I began to realize that no matter what you do in response to a tantrum, you will never, ever, satisfy the disgusted onlookers. That's when I realized that I should completely focus on dealing with my son, exclusively, and completely ignore those who demanded a quick-fix solution. I work out what has triggered the tantrum – hunger, thirst, tiredness, insecurity – and then speak it out.

It's helpful to know that a tantrum is not 'pure badness' as some would suggest but a desperate need to communicate that something is wrong – without the language to do so effectively.

In my case I often say things like, 'I know you're hungry, let's hurry home and have something really nice for dinner.' Or, 'You must be feeling tired. Let's walk slowly and then you can have a sleep when we get home.'

Sometimes there's no reasoning and very little a person can do about a tantrum. Like the incident with the white spirit – we couldn't buy it for him. Similar situations arise in shops where a child wants a sweet or a comic and wants it that moment! Once I say no I try to stick to it – there was a serious tantrum the first time but they were less frequent when my children saw that the message was clear. I take them out of the shop, keep them clear of danger, ignore the stares of strangers and let them get on with it.

As the health visitor once advised me, 'The best way to deal with tantrums is to avoid situations in which they'll happen.' For me that means keeping to a regular routine, not attempting too much when a child is tired or hungry, buying treats when they're not around and presenting them at home as a reward for good behaviour or just a surprise; always carrying a drink and something to eat and listening when they say, 'I'm tired, I want to go home.'

From the very beginning I didn't put my children into

the toys outside shops or buy ice creams from the ice cream van purely because those treats are very public and when you haven't the resources to maintain that treat, the response is very public, too. (I actually didn't plan this approach – we simply couldn't afford these treats at that time and so the children didn't bother asking for them.)

I don't believe that aggressive or violent responses are the right way to deal with irrational behaviour. 'A good smack' neither solves the situation nor is a just solution. Small children have rights and are as entitled to justice as adults. They have a right to be loved, helped and steered through this difficult stage in their lives.

When a child is in the middle of a tantrum, especially in a public place, we may feel as though we're caught up in a situation, like a storm, over which we're powerless.

———

'And leaving the crowd behind, they took him [Jesus], just as he was, in the boat, and there were other boats with him. Then it began to blow a gale and the waves were breaking into the boat so that it was almost swamped. But he was in the stern, his head on the cushion, asleep. They woke him and said to him, "Master do you not care? We are going down!" And he woke up and rebuked the wind and said to the sea, "Quiet now! Be calm!" and the wind dropped and all was calm again.'

Matthew 4:36–39

Jesus didn't panic in the storm – his air of authority and assuredness helped to overcome the storm. When we feel we're swamped and powerless, it helps to have faith and confidence in Jesus to help calm the little storm in our lives.

In the beatitudes, Jesus says, 'Blessed are the gentle...' 'Blessed are the peacemakers...' There are many, many parents who are indeed blessed as they strive to be gentle peacemakers.

———

'I get very cross sometimes when my child has a tantrum. I used to shout at him a lot, but since I have attended church I feel I have more patience with him.'

Kar-li

———

'My faith helps when the children have tantrums. I pray for my anger to be taken away, that I may deal lovingly with the children and I pray for more patience.'

Carmel

———

'My faith has helped me to turn away from the instinctive rough or harsh response to temper tantrums and talk to the child at a calmer time about their behaviour.'

Kate

———

'Some parents find it helps to hold their child quite firmly, until the tantrum passes. This usually only works when

your child is more upset than angry and when you yourself are feeling calm and able to talk gently and reassuringly.'

Birth to Five, Health Education Authority, 1998, p. 63

———

'My faith has helped me to understand that anger should not be disciplined out of a child...'

Amanda

———

'I try to love my children through the difficult patches by remembering the high esteem in which Jesus held little children.'

Margaret

Despite all the advice I have received over the years, there are times when my child has a tantrum and I do get angry. Later, when everything has calmed down and we're talking about what has happened, my little boy says, 'I was very cranky earlier on, Mummy.'

'Yes, you were,' I agree. 'Why were you so cranky?'

'I don't know but *you* were cranky, too.' Yes, I was, but I have no excuse – I'm not three years old and unable to express myself properly.

Once again, the voice of wisdom comes from the child. Our anger also has to be controlled so that toddlers really learn how to cope with this most difficult of emotions.

Five

I Was Sick and You Visited Me...

'I was sick. With teething and wind, with bouts of flu and temperatures and measles and chicken pox and constant colds. And you comforted me, and you lost your sleep, and you were anxious and worried and suffered along with me and stayed off work and cared for me, and I experienced you at your loving best, tender and caring and full of compassion for me. And I knew then how unconditional your love was when I was at my most helpless, and I thought to myself, "Who else would love like this, so selflessly and with such self-sacrifice!" I love you for that. Thank you.'

Michael and Terri Quinn, *From Pram to Primary School*, p. 59

'The path seems less steep when a friend goes along, and the path is easier when the friend is Christ...

*His words must come as a welcome balm to parents:
"Come to me all you that are weary and are carrying
heavy burdens and I will give you rest." To people
exhausted because they stayed up all night with a sick
child and still got to work on time the next morning,
he doesn't offer another challenge. He promises rest.'*

Kathy Coffey, *Experiencing God With Your Children*, p. 143

When I was seven, I felt a sharp pain in the side of my
abdomen while running around the school playground. I
sought solace from my class teacher, a woman very
experienced in the time-wasting techniques of all children.
She told me to sit on the wall and stop making a fuss. As
the pain became more intense and the tears trickled down
my face, I longed for the comforting arms of my parents. I
didn't understand how anyone could ignore my pain and
discomfort. Later that evening I was rushed to hospital
with appendicitis.

Whenever I see the low wall of that playground, I can
almost feel the pain and the coldness I encountered for
feeling ill. All I wanted was to be hugged and reassured
but all I experienced was the cold shoulder of indifference
and the feeling that I was time-wasting. It was an
experience which affected my attitude to children as a
teacher. Once, a normally placid boy threw over his desk

and cursed the whole class because he had a bad pain in his chest. He eventually walked out of the classroom and made his own way to the hospital – he had a collapsed lung. I hope I listened to his suffering – I think I did.

When my own children are ill I think back to my childhood experience of sickness – the care and compassion I received any time I complained of a pain or an ache. My parents never dismissed any discomfort or anxiety, for with children it isn't always possible to tell what is their true physical condition.

The first time our eldest child was ill, we were overwrought with anxiety. He had a cold and it seemed as though he couldn't breathe; he wouldn't stop crying as if there was something seriously wrong with him. He writhed about all over the carpet and, worse than that, he refused to eat his tea. In the early evening we called the doctor.

It wasn't our usual doctor and he looked harassed and annoyed as he burst into the house. 'I was just sitting down to tea with my family,' he said. The unspoken, 'and so this better be worth it…' hung in the air. As he examined our baby, he asked: 'First child?'

'Yes,' we mumbled, quietened by the fear of every possible illness going, particularly meningitis, which had affected several children in our home town around that time.

His face changed, he smiled gently. 'He's fine,' he said. The tension and annoyance fell from his shoulders. 'He has a cold and as it's his first cold, he's feeling terrible and he's just letting you know. There's absolutely nothing to worry about. Keep him cool and give him pain relief every few hours. I understand how you feel – it can be quite alarming when your child is ill for the first time.'

'Thank God!' I whispered. Then it struck me: in all the hours that I had been desperately worried about my baby, all the time I had tried to cool and comfort him, I never once turned to God for help and healing. I never considered that prayer might help to allay my feelings, the Lord, my comforter had never once been called upon.

It isn't so for other parents, as I discovered when I asked how faith helped them to cope with a child's ill-health:

———

'I pray over the children for their healing.'

———

'I do get very worried each time he's not well and I always pray for his health and hope he'll get better soon.'

———

'We always pray for our daughter when she's ill but I think Calpol is wonderful.'

———

'I prayed with my children, especially when they had chicken pox.'

But what exactly do we pray for? If I'm totally honest, the first step to healing my child is to ask the Lord to give me strength and confidence; to stop me from feeling frightened, to believe that my child will be well again. Then I call out, 'Lord, make my child better.'

As I am comforted and reassured by the advice of doctors and the prayers of my wider family, so I try to bring comfort to my sick child. When children are at their most vulnerable, through sickness, it is then that we rediscover their value, their worth. Pre-school children often become babies once again when they're sick. They want to be cuddled all the time, they yearn for food that's easily digestible and they don't like to be far away from Mummy or Daddy.

When we have to carry them around or stay beside them, it's physically hard and mentally stressful, but the way we treat them shapes their attitude to sickness and vulnerability in the future.

When I am ill with the flu or a bad cold I long for a good sleep or a few hours' peace. My children, however, have other ideas – they want to stay beside me, wipe my brow with a cool flannel and read to me. They want to kiss and cuddle me until I'm better. It's hard to cope with all this but, on reflection, I'm pleased that they want to help me.

There are times when it feels our society is one which

despises illness and weakness. Many firms no longer pay their employees when they're away from work because of illness. The old and vulnerable are tidied away in the corners of our cities, in homes where we can forget about their dependency on us. This isn't a good model for our children and that's one of the reasons why it's so good for parents to treat their children with great love and kindness when they are at their weakest.

Recovery can bring its problems, too. Just after our oldest child started school, he fell victim to one of the many viruses affecting children. The first twenty-four hours were very worrying as he was so lethargic with a particularly high temperature. Then, on the second day, he asked for a bed downstairs and books to look at. We made a fuss of him, brought a portable bed downstairs and surrounded him with activities suitable for a convalescing child. We tempted his palate with his favourite food, not worrying too much about him having a balanced diet.

That evening, as we prayed, we talked about the best things in our day. 'The best part of my day,' he said, his voice still croaking, 'was being sick.'

'Why?' we asked, puzzled.

'Because I had lots of cuddles and loads of stories.'

This was our boy talking about how good it was to be sick. Where do we go wrong, if our children have to be ill before we show them how much we really love them? 'Lots of cuddles and loads of stories.' This should have been an everyday feature of life in our household but it wasn't.

I was well, fighting fit and you didn't play with me.

Six

Refusing to Feast

'The most important item of furniture in a Christian home is the meal table.'

'For a Christian, meal times are the Eucharistic feast for the family.'

I heard both of these statements many years ago and I nodded at the wisdom and comfort within those words. At the time, I thought back to the large dining table of my childhood home and the lovely meals we shared there. It is only since my own children have arrived that I realize how selective and romantic memory can be.

There were many, many happy times around our dining table but then there were arguments and disagreements, too. There must have been times, although I can't remember any, when food was refused and pushed away. It certainly wasn't one long Eucharistic feast, or holy meal together.

The early days of feeding my children were simple and straightforward. I felt great joy at the weight they gained and the changes in their physique, simply from my own breast milk. For me, it was a tremendous miracle in itself and it felt like a wonderful achievement. After the pain and discomfort of the early stages, nourishing them on a regular basis also brought me great comfort.

Then to weaning. It's generally accepted that this is a difficult stage and so it seemed, at first. Then both of the children took to the mashed carrot and baby rice with a voracious appetite. Before every bowl of stewed fish and cabbage, we said grace and thanked God for his goodness. 'It is nutritious,' I chanted to myself, 'even though the smell is disgusting.'

Mealtimes were a pleasure, if a little messy, until the first-born reached the age of two and a half. Then he began to discover the power of refusing to eat. Not only did it make Mummy cross and upset, the repercussions seemed to last for hours.

The refusals started with egg sandwiches. 'I'm not eating those,' he said. 'They're disgusting!' and he pushed his plate into the middle of the table. Then stew received the same treatment, then pizza, pasta, sausages, chips, fish fingers. As I prepared each meal he would walk into the kitchen and sing out a litany of all the types of food which were forbidden. Eventually, he became anxious about what we would cook – one of the first questions he would ask in the morning would be, 'What's for dinner today?'

I was emotionally very hurt. I love cooking and it has always given me great pleasure to see my meals eaten and enjoyed. To witness my own son dismiss my cooking – without tasting it – in such an irreverent manner hurt me deeply. Our home Eucharistic table was no more. Now we were the site of a nutritional battlefield.

'Try a little,' was met with, 'No! It smells disgusting.'

'But you'll be hungry.'

'No I won't, I'm having a banana.'

'No dinner, no banana!'

'All right then.'

We tried every bribe and every type of sweet talking. Even Weetabix was dismissed at one stage. Then I began to realize that our daily diet had diminished to about four dishes to accommodate the very restricted tastes of our son. I was concerned about this, even though we were eating a nutritionally balanced diet. In many parts of the world, children have no choice over what they eat – indeed many children go without food.

In Kenya, some years ago, the children told me how much they loved their Ugali – a type of porridge made with maize meal. I tried it a few times and, like my son, dismissed it with a turned-up nose and an offended palate.

'How can you eat it?' I asked. 'It is our food – we love it,' the children replied, laughing at my strange tastes.

For those children there were no alternatives to Ugali and certainly no snacks in between meals. If you're hungry, even the same food eaten every day tastes delicious. Maybe we give our children too much choice, too much food. Remembering the children of Solai in Kenya, I began to have more patience with my own son.

Eating, like praying, walking, speaking and every other skill, has to be approached with gentleness. Babies and small children need to develop respect for food. This may mean cutting out all snacks so that when they arrive at the family feast they are genuinely hungry and ready to eat. Indeed, when there are children who die of starvation because of the greed of others – is it right to encourage our children to eat between meals?

It's important to remember that meal times are just that – a meal, not feeding time. So it's good to remove all distractions, like the television.

———

'The Eucharist must seem foreign to children who eat meals in front of television sets. To appreciate it, they need the experience of sitting around a table where failure and fruitfulness sit close enough to pass the butter…'

Kathy Coffey, *Experiencing God With Your Children*, pp. 93–94

At the beginning of each meal, it helps to invite God to be a guest and, with the children, to say a prayer of blessing on the food. Sometimes this establishes an atmosphere and it says, 'This meal is important – not just to us but also to the Lord.'

We also bless and welcome visitors to our meal in the grace. Granny and Pop are the main recipients of this blessing and the children look so delighted to welcome guests in this special way.

Even before the meal begins, involving children with the preparation can help to overcome any difficulties at the table. Making a meal of the preparation can help children to appreciate the importance of sitting down and eating together.

———

'We try to make our meals a joint venture: with suitable knives, the boys help to chop the vegetables for the meal. One of the boys sets the table and we all help to carry the food to the table. I think one of the reasons I've had very few problems with eating is that the boys want to know if they're eating the vegetables they have chopped. Because my boys are involved in the making of almost every meal, they have respect for food and our meal times are fairly peaceful and harmonious.'

Kate, mother of three boys aged two to seven years

In her children's book, *A Quiet Night In*, Jill Murphy has the children making postcards for their parents' special meal. They also spend time decorating the table for their father's birthday celebration. It's an idea which could catch on. If we go to a very special meal, like a wedding or anniversary celebration, there are often name cards to show us where we should sit.

Why do we limit such practices to special times, often outside of the home? If we are important, if we believe that we are made in God's image, then we can have a special meal, an occasion in our own home. There are many reasons for a celebration – one of them could be simply celebrating our own family. The children could be involved in the preparation of the meal, making name cards and table decorations, placing a good cloth on the table and cooking food which we know will be appreciated. Take time over the meal, enjoy one another's company. Careful preparation cuts down on some interruptions, for example, taking a child to the toilet immediately prior to the meal and having jugs of juice and water on the table, along with wine if it's a major celebration!

Let the children know that this is a special meal and treat them with dignity and courtesy throughout – they are honoured guests. Make time for a special blessing on the meal, perhaps something the children have composed themselves. In the grace, bless each member of the family sitting at the table and say something positive about their contribution to the meal – without allowing the food to go cold.

This isn't something which can be attempted every day – you need to have plenty of time and be in a relaxed frame of mind. However, it can be a really powerful experience. We have tried this and there are very few eating problems at an important meal such as this. It isn't a cure-all and there will still be days when mealtimes are like battlefields. It does, however, make the dining table the Eucharistic feast of the family, its spiritual centre – if only for a few hours every week.

Then, there are other problems to be looked to – after all, we are only human.

Seven

Training the Unmentionable

What is a spiritual approach to toilet training, for goodness' sake? Isn't it just the same for everybody in every race, creed and nation on earth? Everybody has to... well, they do, don't they? So what is this chapter doing in this book? It bears no earthly relevance to faith.

Except it does. Listen to the tale of one mother:

'We found toilet training, initially, very easy – at just past his second birthday. Then a bug made my little boy ill for several weeks. For ages after this we faced constant constipation and occasional messing. I found it so frustrating especially when it happened five minutes after we'd left the house. I became extremely irritated, even more so when the condition became worse. I felt as though he was doing it on purpose, probably to gain attention.

Days when we'd had a good clear-out were like days of real celebration and he was such a different boy. When he was all bunged up and messing himself, my little boy was bad-tempered and very, very unhappy. Any adult would know the discomfort and pain of prolonged constipation. Why then was it so hard for me to be kind to my little boy?

The constant writhing about in agony followed by unhappy hours sitting on the toilet with no results followed by soiled clothes, only minutes later, became very difficult to bear. This was harming my relationship with my child. Advice and help were sought. From family, friends and professionals the words were the same: "Be patient, he'll soon grow out of it. Be kind when he messes himself and tell him not to worry, otherwise he'll get a complex."

But I couldn't be kind and I had lost my patience. I was horrible to him and when I look back now, I'm ashamed of the way I behaved at such a critical time in his life.

Then one Sunday, at church, the preacher said this: "I want you to place your prayers before the Lord. Ask him for his help in your life. If there's a problem or an area of your life where you're unhappy, let the Lord help. Remember, no problem is too small for the Lord, nothing too trivial. You can't embarrass or shock him."

Those words reverberated around my brain and I spoke a quiet, desperate prayer: "Lord, help my child to use the toilet properly. Help me to love him, especially when he messes himself. Help me to be gentle and loving when I'm cleaning him. Give me strength and patience when I feel angry and annoyed."

From that very day things started to improve. It's one of those miracles which people are often afraid to mention. I felt trusting in the Lord had given me confidence to do the right thing.'

Other parents find praying with their children, even when they're on the toilet, helps the child to relax.

———

'I pray for the healing of problems and I teach my children to pray for themselves, e.g. "Please Jesus, don't let my poo have sharp edges"!'

Prayer helps at those difficult moments in our lives when we feel we can't cope any more, like the mother who was at the end of her tether. These are times to place our trust in God, and also to look at the whole person and ask and listen for advice.

———

'I never stopped praying about my little boy's problem but I sensed there was something wrong with his diet. After the episode where I prayed we had another time when our little boy didn't go to the toilet for about a fortnight. The doctor I consulted recommended that I examine his diet.

Over a few days I realized that he was eating very little fibre – he didn't like vegetables. Someone suggested prune juice and fresh orange juice. These worked and we haven't had any problems since he has been taking these regularly. It reminds me of a poster we once saw outside a Baptist church: "If you're caught in a storm, pray… but don't stop rowing!"'

Many people underestimate the unhappiness toilet problems can bring to a family. The mother of a child with special needs acknowledges this:

———

'With my little girl I find this very difficult and it is the one thing that would make our lives so much easier but at the moment it is very hard. I know it will happen eventually.'

Every single area of our life is important to God. He understands our struggles to raise our children with kindness and patience. But he cares for us. He knows the numbers of hairs on our head, he can account for every sparrow. Our worries are his worries and nothing, as the preacher said, is too trivial for him to care about.

Many pre-school play groups use toilet training as a bench mark for acceptance. A child has to be 'clean and dry' before they will be enrolled. In France, a child can start school as soon as she is toilet-trained. For many, this is but more pressure in a stressful situation. For parents of children with special needs who strive to lead their children towards independence, it can make life miserable.

Trusting in God and praying for his healing and support in this area of life can help, along with the care of friends and family.

It's wonderful when a gentle, patient approach pays off with our children and it's magical when they reflect that goodness back to us. Like the day my son noticed that our visitor was missing from the room. 'Mummy, where has Rita gone?' he asked.

'She's just nipped up to the loo,' I replied, quietly.

'Is she all right? She's been gone a long time. Will she need someone to massage her tummy?' This was a method we had been advised to use when our child had constipation. It worked.

That's one of the times I see God working through my little boy.

> Lord, help my mummy
> when she massages my tummy
> and make me better.

You see, there is a spiritual approach to toilet training.

Eight

Play With Me, Play With Me – A Spiritual Approach to Toys

Hamleys, the famous London toy shop, announced record sales in the pre-Christmas rush one year recently. More independent observers noted the levels of tension and aggression in the shop in the run-up to the festive season. Parents, desperate for the *in* toy for their child, wrestled with other adults in their efforts to secure a purchase. Sharp words and menacing body language became part of the seasonal rush.

As I write, we are hurtling towards another Christmas, and another stampede is under way for this year's *in* toy. Newspapers report the fights and harsh words exchanged in queues as people wait, from the early hours, to purchase one of these precious items.

Designer label toys, along with trademark clothes, have become the new status symbols for fashion-conscious parents. This is the advice of a 'Toy Expert' writing in a local paper: 'The best quality toys are usually the most expensive...' He did add that they usually last longer.

From a very young age, there is pressure on parents to have just the right toy for their child. At about three months old people start asking, 'Have you got a baby gym for your child to play with on the floor?' Then it's the cot activity centre and the buggy activity centre and the precious teddy, then the right sort of rattles and feely toys...

Walking through town recently, I was amazed at the number of toys attached to buggies. What was even more interesting was the fact that not one of the babies was playing with these beautiful, bright toys – the bright lights and constant changing of faces, people and scenery were enough to amuse even the most active baby.

So why do we spend so much money on toys and time deliberating over what is the right object for our child? As a Christian, I question the morality of buying so many toys for our children. What are we really doing? Are we training them, from a very early age, to be conspicuous consumers? Are we educating them in capitalism and materialism?

In our family we have consciously tried not to buy too

many toys for our children. At first this was for personal economic reasons: we simply couldn't afford them. Now we don't feel comfortable buying whatever our children demand, especially if it's in response to peer pressure – yes, this now starts at about two and a half years old. However, a visitor from a developing country once remarked on the number of toys and books in our home.

———

'Back home, our children tend to play with toys they have made themselves from waste material or toys their parents have made. A whole village of children would have a field day in your house with all these toys.'

There's another question for the Christian to ask about toys. What are they for? I know, I know – they're for children to play with but what are they really for? Be honest, are they to develop and stimulate our child or are they to keep them busy and out of our way? Then we can get on with much more important things like cooking or cleaning, reading the paper, chatting to friends on the phone or watching television. Are we attracted to toys which are advertised as 'Guaranteed to keep your child amused for hours'? Is that what we really want?

Then there's the problem of Christmas. Are we like the pushy parents in pre-Christmas Hamleys – aggressive and menacing in our search for the perfect toy for our child? Is this the right way to prepare for the birth of Jesus? What message do we give about our faith when we celebrate with our children in such a materialistic fashion?

Then there's the question of what we give our children. I personally have a problem with many of the toys available. I am uncomfortable about my children wanting to play with guns, swords or knives. I don't like them playing with figures whose main function is to be aggressive or combative. Many ask, what harm can these toys do to children? It's impossible to say – my brothers had toy guns and they have grown into non-violent, gentle men. However, the climate is different now. There have been so many atrocities involving the use of guns. How can we consider them to be toys?

Recently I have begun to question whether it's right for them to play with so many cars. (Am I preparing them to be passive drivers rather than active walkers?) In constructing a road, bridge and a traffic jam across the front room, am I saying that this is the way life is and it will never change? Living in an area where the volume of traffic causes health problems and restrictions on our lives, I wonder how long it will be before cars will become unfashionable toys.

I also feel very uncomfortable with electronic and computerized toys. Many of them are very expensive, they have little appeal and they don't allow a child to use her imagination. I find the noises they emit rather offensive, too. One of the most important functions of a toy is to help develop a child's imagination. If all the work is done for the child, then the toy has very little use.

What about the big outdoor toys? Since the day in the 1980s when politicians told us, 'There is no such thing as society,' there has been a considerable growth in the number of adventure playgrounds in back gardens. These days, every self-respecting toddler has a climbing frame, sandpit, slide, paddling pool, bike, tractor, car and swing in their play space. Unfortunately, the community play facilities are under-used, neglected and may soon be abandoned. Only the rich kids have fun. Having said all that, my children have benefited enormously from the generosity of parents who have shared their summer back gardens with us and many others. Children of parents like these will grow into generous and giving adults.

Everything we do and everything we buy communicates a message to our children. Could that message be, 'In order to be happy, you need to spend lots of money on bright, noisy, attractive things'? If that's the message we are communicating to our children then it's a poor thing for our society. Are we also teaching our children to be demanding and greedy, as we give in to their every request and desire?

There's another way and it applies to people of all faiths.

A Health Visitor once said to me, 'You are the greatest toy for your baby.' What a lift to a parent's self-esteem, to hear words such as these. But it's true – babies love to watch their parents' faces when they're talking, they love to be involved in the activity of the house. It's great entertainment.

Parents need to have confidence in themselves to play with their children. Toys are important but they need to be chosen carefully. Children can only play with one toy at a time so there's no need for boxes and boxes of toys. As early as possible, children need to learn how to share their toys – in that way toys are not seen as precious possessions with an end in themselves but as tools for learning how to share and how to have fun.

———

'Think of the lilies, they neither spin nor sow.'
Matthew 6:28

Developing the imagination helps to interpret the world, God's creation. It's hard for children to do this through toys which don't develop imaginative or creative skills. Here, the parents' role in playing with their children becomes very important.

If we give young children expensive toys which we hope will keep them busy and out of our way for hours, then we'll feel annoyed and frustrated when they tire of the toy within a few minutes. We may also feel they're being ungrateful for something that has cost a lot of money. However, if we spend time positively playing with our children, giving them good, quality time – where we enjoy ourselves as much as they do – it will make a big difference to our lives, as well as theirs.

After completing the parenting course, I placed this little poem in a prominent place in my kitchen.

> I hope my children look back on today
> And see a parent who had time to play.
> There will be years for cleaning and cooking
> But children grow up when you're not looking.
> So quiet down cobwebs, dust go to sleep,
> I'm rocking my baby and babies don't keep.

Author unknown, quoted in Michael and Terri Quinn,
From Pram to Primary School, p. 51

Adopting a less materialistic and less acquisitive approach to the development of play and imagination provides a model of justice and equity for our children. We can show them that fun and enjoyment do not depend on how much money we spend in the toy shop. In a fair world, where our children are really considered as important, there would be no queues at the toy shop; indeed, there may be little need for toy shops at all.

Nine

Going to Church

*'Every week, in my search for heaven,
I go through hell!'*

The words of a mother who struggles through a weekly church service with two small children. Why is it so hellish, to bring our babies, our little bits of the divine, to church?

———

'I set off with good intentions every week. I think, "I'll be patient and kind, I'll try not to bribe or cajole or threaten them if they're restless." Then they ask to go to the toilet – I take them out, trying not to cause too much of a stir. Five minutes later they ask to go again. No, you've just been! I'll hiss to them. But I need to go again! This used to be repeated all the way through the service. Then they'd start climbing over the pews, running around, shouting, asking for drinks. If there are other children nearby, they seem to

compete with one another to see who's the noisiest and the naughtiest.

One Sunday, after a particularly difficult time, another parishioner stopped me on the way out of church. "Can't you do anything to control your children?" he asked. "They're so distracting during the service. Why don't you make them sit still?"

I walked home feeling angry, humiliated and inadequate. In my mind I replied to his question. "Yes, I can control them. I have a little box in my pocket with two red buttons which emit high frequency signals, controlling their movements. The only thing is, it doesn't work in church."

For a few more weeks after that I went to church but I never felt the same again. It was as though other parishioners were watching me, thinking how inadequate I was as a parent. If anything, the children's behaviour got worse, so I just stopped going.'

How terribly sad that a parent with such good intentions is lost to the Christian community because of a careless remark.

I've had similar experiences to this, although I've never been told that I should control my children a little more. On bad Sundays when the children have been particularly energetic and vocal, I've asked my mother how she made us behave in church. (There were eight of us and along with our parents, we took up a whole pew at the front of church.) 'You wouldn't dare misbehave,' is all my mother says.

'What's the secret? How did you make us behave?' I ask but no more advice is given in this area. I can still remember the tap on the back and the warning finger if we shuffled about, fidgeted or failed to kneel up straight. That was nothing compared with the way my children and their contemporaries behave. Beyond 'You wouldn't dare...' there is little advice from my mother. Other members of her generation tut loudly when they hear my eldest child ask questions like, 'Can Jesus hear us if we sit right back here?' Or, 'Why are the toilets locked during Mass? I need a pee!'

It's important to examine exactly what we're asking of our children on a Sunday morning in many churches up and down the country. First of all, in many places, we ask them to sit on a wooden pew or in a confined space for at least an hour. We want them to sit still in that space and play quietly. Then, we want them to listen to adult voices speaking continuously, with no visual aids and only occasional breaks for music for an hour or even more. If they become restless, we become nervous and agitated. We whisper and hiss at them using tones we wouldn't normally employ in the rest of the week. We bribe them, 'If you're good and sit still for an hour I'll buy you some chocolate on the way home.' We threaten them, 'Sit still now, get down from there now or I'll...' We cajole them in a strained, tense voice. 'Come on now, sit up here and try to be good.'

Is this what we really want for our children? Is their first taste of community worship marred by bribes and threats and tensions? Is this what Jesus would want for them and for us?

Sometimes when I reflect on how hard it can be at church on Sunday, I try to imagine how it would have been for those listening to Jesus as he preached to the five thousand. There are no parish statistics for those times but I'm sure that a good many of the throng would have been children. After a while they would have tired of sitting still on a rocky hillside and so played and ran around within their parents' orbit. Even though they would have been entranced by the words of Jesus, the adults would also have stood up, stretched their legs and yawned. Their stomachs would have rumbled, too.

Two thousand years later, things are very different. How did it happen, in the building of our churches, chapels and cathedrals, that we made so little floor space available for worshippers, especially children.

Within our places of worship there is a place for stillness and quiet but there's also room for noise and brightness and activity. In the past few years, many churches have recognized the need to welcome and accommodate babies and children in a much more positive way. In our own parish, there's a crèche and a children's liturgy group at one of the services.

Even in places where the liturgy and facilities aren't child friendly, we can be surprised at how much children feel at home. In the summer we visited a local Cistercian Monastery for Mass and it was one of the most peaceful Sunday mornings we have experienced with our two children. Later, we talked about why they had been so attentive – what did they like about it? What made them so still and reflective? Was it the early morning summer sunshine, bursting into the monastery church like a natural, beaming spotlight? Or was it the incense floating high into the shafts of sunshine, drifting through the congregation? Or the confident singing of the monks, or simply the whole beautiful spectacle? I think it was a combination of all those things – their senses were well and truly exercised that day.

Whatever it was, it made a welcome change from the Sundays when we have to restrain both of the children with their toy doctor's set, asking a neighbouring parishioner, 'Can I check your chest, please?' (Maybe we shouldn't have allowed them to bring the toy stethoscope to Mass.)

Children are very important people in the church. They

have been bribed and threatened for long enough. There should be no more tuts of disapproval or negative remarks made to parents. It's hard enough getting a family ready for church and being there on time without being criticized for nothing more than a child's exuberance.

Many churches recognize this and in the next section of this book we will look at the range of facilities available to the parents of babies and children.

If you're still thinking about community faith for your child, read on! You'll be pleasantly surprised.

Church and Chapel

How Churches
Welcome Children

One

Whatever Has Happened to Our Sabbath?

There was a time when almost everyone went to church on Sunday. It was a traditional time for people to attend church and Sunday school. Now, Sundays are very different. The Sabbath has changed quite dramatically. Whatever has happened?

Recently I watched a children's television programme about a Jewish family celebrating the Shabat. I was so impressed with their adherence to the tenets of their faith: their refusal to do any work on the Sabbath; their lovely meals; their relaxing together, the unity, the quietness and peace of their home.

I compared this with our own Sabbath. On Sundays we rush our breakfast, then to church, visit the relatives and then rush home. There are many options open to us, shopping among them. But as we take our Sunday afternoon walk to the park or to the allotment, I am amazed at the number of cars on the road. Often, I feel as though I want to cry out, 'Stop it – stop moving about, stop rushing! Be quiet and calm and peaceful – if only for a few minutes.'

We may have gained a great deal through our shops and supermarkets being open on Sundays: the chance for families to shop together (although I can think of a hundred things I'd rather do with my family!) the acknowledgment of a multi-cultural society which has more than one Sabbath, and the ability to choose exactly when we can shop.

It seems, however, that we have lost a great deal more than we have gained. We have lost our chance to pause, to reflect, to enjoy recreation. That's the whole point of the Sabbath – to stop, look back on a week of creation and to look forward to beginning again the next morning. As parents of small children, we really need that space in our busy lives.

On weekdays, even on Saturdays, there is a focal point for our day. There's work or searching for work; taking the children to school, shopping, going to Mums and Toddlers group, visiting friends. But Sundays, ah… Sundays, it's one of those 'What shall we do with all those free hours?' sort of days.

At other times, in another age, church was the focal point

for Sundays. For as far back as I can remember, going to Mass was the main feature of our Sunday. When I was very young I think it was something we all had to get out of the way, then we could get on with the rest of the day.

The Sabbath was a day of rest, but only for some in the household. The women had to work twice as hard, first of all preparing the children for church, washed and dressed in their best clothes, and later cooking a roast dinner. Then there was all the clearing up. It wasn't all roses and recreation in days gone by but there did seem to be fewer stresses and complications.

As a new parent, Sundays made me think of my uncle – a farmer in the West of Ireland. 'A day of rest? You must be joking – the cows still have to be milked, the hens fed and the milk delivered.' It's the same with a baby – the nappies still have to be changed, the clothes washed (or there's an unmanageable pile on Mondays), and the children have to be fed. Babies can't distinguish between five o'clock on a Sunday morning and the same time on a Monday morning.

So how do parents manage to make Sundays a bit different, a little more special, so that we recognize the Sabbath at the end or beginning of our week? Those of us who strive to live a good life, inspired by Christian principles, sometimes find it easy to forget about the Sabbath, the Lord's Day, which we are instructed to keep holy.

How can we keep the Sabbath? First of all, we can look at when Christians believe the Sabbath was instituted:

——

'On the seventh day God completed the work he had been doing. God blessed the seventh day and made it holy, because on that day he had rested after all his work of creating.'

Genesis 2:1–3

God made the Sabbath a day of rest, a day for rest. Jesus helped to clarify the true meaning of the Sabbath when he was challenged by the Pharisees:

——

'… The Pharisees said to him, "Look, why are they doing something on the Sabbath day that is forbidden?" and he replied… "The Sabbath was made for man, not man for the Sabbath…"'

Mark 2:27

The Sabbath was made for us. What a gift! A whole twenty-four hours in which we can rest, take our time, reflect on how our lives are going, enjoy one another's company and make a little space for God. Yes, the children still have to be washed and fed but they can be enjoyed, too. That's what the Sabbath is for.

There are very simple ways for making the Sabbath day

different, a day set apart. These are ways which help parents and small children to appreciate one another. When I was small, porridge was for weekdays and cornflakes for the weekends. I thought cornflakes were a treat – I didn't realize until years later that it was to cut down the work for my mother on Saturdays and Sundays.

That's one way of starting the Sabbath differently – an unusual breakfast which automatically sets the day apart from all others. We can take our time over breakfast on the Sabbath – we don't have to rush to work or school or to our various groups.

We can allow others to enjoy their Sabbath, too. This may mean restricting our activities. If we want to shop at supermarkets and garden centres on a Sunday then we restrict the freedom to rest of those who work in such places. Many people say, 'It's the only time we have to shop together.' But is it, really? It may be the time we *choose* to shop together. How did we all manage before Sunday opening?

Shopping as a family? My children may be different from others – they can endure shopping for about ten minutes. Trailing from shop to shop is a boring activity for children. There are many more ways to enjoy their company, which we'll explore later in the book.

Sunday shopping brings a busyness and noisiness to the streets which makes it like any other day. How long will it be before there is no break in our working week? For the families of those who work in the retail trade, this is the reality already. Is this what we want on the Lord's Day for the Lord's people?

Parents of babies and small children need, more than ever, a time to rest, a time to reflect. They need special moments – like a good dinner on the Sabbath, cooked together to ease the burden of the work. They need space to enjoy that meal. They need an opportunity to meet other like-minded parents in a community setting. This opportunity is provided by many of our churches on a Sunday morning.

Jesus said, 'Come to me, all you who labour, and I will give you rest' (Matthew 11:28–30). He gave us rest, a great gift, and look what we've done with it. Yet, there is another way, a way to appreciate the gift of the Sabbath. A way to rest for a moment and allow ourselves to be recreated.

Two

What Is the Point of Going to Church on Sunday?

Many, many parents would like to attend church on Sunday mornings; they strive to do something to make the Sabbath different. For those who try it isn't easy and sometimes they find themselves asking the question, 'What is the point of going to church on Sundays?' I must confess that there have been times when I have puzzled over this. I have often woken in the middle of the night and wondered why, exactly, I spend more than an hour struggling and writhing with my two small children every Sunday.

'To hear the word of God?' Well… sometimes I hear nothing apart from the screams of protest from the two little ones. I hear neither the word of God, nor the word of the priest or reader. As we travel home from Mass I often wonder why I hadn't stayed at home, given the children something to keep them quiet for twenty minutes and read the scripture readings quietly to myself.

'To praise the Lord?' Well... I try but most of my mutterings on a Sunday morning are not words of praise. Threats, bribes, pleadings, yes – but not praise. Sometimes I sense that I hear the thoughts of other parishioners as they look towards us and other parents struggling with small children. I can almost see the loud tuts inside their foreheads, their faces betraying the criticism they feel.

'Years ago, children behaved themselves at church...' I have heard that from many people over the last four years. I understand their frustration but their words only serve to make many parents feel inadequate and angry. Years ago children did behave themselves at church – I can't argue with that; I remember kneeling and standing perfectly still for well over an hour. We wouldn't even slouch or lean back when our bodies hurt with tiredness.

What was it that made our parents such wonderful beings? What was it about church and church services that made children so good in the old days? Children 'behaved' not because they were spiritually engaged but because they were frightened of the consequences of not behaving. Fear. We didn't need to be smacked in order to keep us quiet. A warning look shot across the pews was all we needed to remind us about our 'behaviour'.

What has been the result of all that 'good behaviour' in churches thirty years ago? As adults, when the fear had subsided, people simply stopped going to church. As a parent, I am beginning to realize that my children's behaviour at church is not inappropriate. They are not naughty – they are acting and behaving as two- and four-year-olds normally behave. Their behaviour is totally appropriate. Why then do we demand that they sit still, be quiet and listen in a building whose design is neither child-friendly nor interesting?

Recently I have begun to look back at the 'halcyon' days of my childhood without rose-coloured spectacles. Yes, we sat still and were quiet for over an hour each Sunday morning but that was not being well-behaved. If anything, our behaviour was inappropriate for small children.

For a parent, it is a defining moment to realize that our children are not naughty when they move around in church services. We may want them to be quiet and sit still but they want to continue discovering their world. They want to hear how their voice sounds as it moves through the rafters of a church ceiling. They want to feel the wooden, stone or carpeted floor under their feet. They long to touch the bright flowers and watch as the smoke rises from the candles. They can smell the incense and yes, they want to talk, they want to tell you all about what they are hearing, seeing, smelling and touching. There are years and years ahead of us for training children in the way of appropriate behaviour. Infancy is a time for exploration and discovery – that is appropriate behaviour for a small child.

What is the point of going to church on a Sunday if we feel tense and uneasy because others may judge our children's behaviour as inappropriate? Whatever others may think, if we consider ourselves to be Christians, going to church on a Sunday actually sustains us. Our not being there doesn't mean that God will punish us – I cannot believe that God is like that. Being with other Christians on a Sunday will strengthen and encourage us through the rest of the week.

Without us, the Christian community isn't complete:

———

'Just as a human body, though it is made up of many parts, is a single unit because all these parts, though many, make one body, so it is with Christ. In the one spirit we were all baptized, Jews as well as Greeks, slaves as well as citizens, and one spirit was given to us all to drink... Now you together are Christ's body but each of you is a different part of it...'

1 Corinthians 12:12–13, 27

As a child I never, ever questioned our going to church on Sundays. It was simply part of the fabric of our lives.

Although there were bits that I found boring, I loved the spectacle and the music. Then there were the May processions and Corpus Christi processions. As a young adult, my faith was greatly renewed by many of the lecturers and other students at teacher training college. So it was that when I started teaching in a strange town, I knew that I would find a welcome at church on Sundays. Through years of working in places far away from home, church was the one place where I felt I belonged, where I experienced a common bond with other worshippers. If work was difficult, I knew that on a Sunday morning there was a space for reflection and a sense of belonging. I was sustained and nourished by my attendance at church on Sunday mornings.

Nowadays, I feel a valued member of our church community. If we didn't go to church on Sundays, I know that we, as a family, would be missed. I often miss families or individuals who are ill or away on holiday. The community is incomplete; the Body of Christ is not functioning properly in our world. There are those who, for one reason or another, have simply stopped coming to church. It may be that they were hurt by something done or said. Maybe they merely grew tired or bored. Whatever the reasons or circumstances, we need those who have become estranged to return. We miss them – the Christian community isn't the same without them.

Nothing is perfect. There are many times when I question why I'm at church. I think I'm in good company:

———

'… *I still attend church regularly. Part of my motivation is the inability to answer Peter's question to Jesus, "But where else would we go?" No matter how cosy our home or how stunning our mountain scenery, it still doesn't hold a candle to the power of someone laying down his life for us and continuing to feed us with a bread and wine transformed into himself. Despite the frequency of dismal preaching, male-dominated rites, exclusive language, an apathetic assembly, and an unimaginative clergy, something keeps pulling me back.'*

Kathy Coffey, *Experiencing God With Your Children*, pp. 85–86

I'm not always sure what it is but at least we keep going and searching for ways to support others in our parish on Sundays. The same is happening elsewhere. Many churches now have good facilities for babies and small children – they realize that parents need to feel welcome, they want to know that their children are not annoying or irritating other members of the community. Parents need space to hear the word of the Lord and time to reflect on this. They also want to belong to a Christian community so that they may play a full role in the working of the Body of Christ, the Kingdom of God on earth.

The next part of the book describes the excellent facilities for parents and their children in several churches. This is their response to the call of Jesus: 'Suffer little children to come unto me, for theirs is the kingdom of heaven.'

Once the maxim 'Children should be seen and not heard' rang true in many of our communities. Today, children, in all their vitality and joy, are an important presence in the church.

Three

Suffer Little Children...
to Come to Our Church

I wrote to several churches in my neighbourhood and asked about their provision for babies and small children and their parents in order to discover what facilities are available. The responses were very interesting and so I worked out a programme for visiting a different church every Sunday. The first week I was to visit the local Methodist Church where I knew there was good provision for the smaller members of the community. I looked forward to an enjoyable and inspiring Sunday morning in their company.

Sunday morning arrived, grey and damp. The rain spattered against every window and my oldest child had a high temperature. 'What are you going to do?' my husband asked anxiously. It was an easy decision to make – I wanted to be with my sick child so my visit to the

Methodist Church would have to wait for another Sunday.

How often does this sort of thing happen to parents who genuinely want to belong to a church community? Take, for example, somebody who, after attending a Christmas service, makes it a New Year's resolution to start going to church again. The first Sunday in January – the in-laws are visiting and it would be rude to leave them. The following Sunday, the baby is ill and it's not worth the risk of taking her out... then you catch the bug yourself and another Sunday is gone. By the fourth Sunday in January you have lost the parish magazine you picked up after the Christmas morning service so... it's February, you're snowed in, and it's too cold to lift the little one in and out of the car.

It can be very, very hard for a parent to make a decision to go to church. With children things are always happening – in winter they are afflicted by colds and fevers and it stops us from going to church. When they are in good health and the conditions are right, we may have lost the incentive to attend. What we need is somebody who will say, 'Come with me. I'll take you there, I'll be beside you and I will make you welcome.' Life can be difficult enough without having the added stress on a Sunday morning of walking into a strange environment where we know nobody.

I wanted to know, as a mother of two small children, how I would feel as I walked into a new church. How would I be welcomed? How would I cope with two boisterous, energetic children in a new setting where I was a stranger?

The day before I attended a service in one of the churches, I contacted the minister and explained the purpose of my visit. Each Sunday morning for several weeks I visited a different church. I spent some time in the main service and then time in the crèche and in the Sunday school for pre-school children. After the service and the Sunday school, I spoke to the parents about their church and I asked them to complete a simple questionnaire about the childcare provision and other issues concerning parents of small children.

I was greatly encouraged with the many responses I received. On the whole, people were positive about their churches. There is a great deal of hard work taking place on Sunday mornings, on behalf of our children. In the areas of childcare, liturgy and worship, Bible study and support for parents, there is a great deal to rejoice about.

Being a Christian parent demands much more than a weekly visit to church. Faith and spirituality affect every part of a person's being – every action, every thought and every word. But the Sunday visit to church can greatly reinforce what happens at home during the rest of the week. Meeting with other Christians on Sundays helps put everything into perspective. Being in touch with the wider church can support and sustain parents from Monday to Saturday and help to lead children along a safer and surer path through life.

Four

Welcoming

The welcome we receive on arriving at church makes a huge and lasting impression. If we are made to feel as though we are valued individuals, we will want to belong. However, if we are overlooked and ignored, it is hard to feel at home there. A good welcome is vitally important, especially to parents of small children.

———

'Every Sunday I arrive at church totally worn out, as if I have done a day's work. I have four small children and getting them ready or encouraging them to dress themselves is a mammoth task. Then actually getting there, walking or in the car, is another huge event. But the smiles of welcome at the church door, from the minister and other parishioners, make all the effort worthwhile. They truly make us feel welcome and appreciate our effort to be there.'

It isn't easy. Getting children fed, washed and dressed for church is a difficult task on a Sunday morning. It takes commitment and faith. I'm sure there are many who feel that it would be far easier to stay at home. The welcome people receive at the church door can make all the difference.

Some time ago I heard this story about a particular church community. Once there was a man who walked into church wearing his hat. It was a smart, grey trilby. He sat in a pew halfway down the church and began to pray. After a few moments, a woman tapped him on the shoulder. 'Do you mind,' she said indignantly. 'You're supposed to remove your hat in church.'

'Well, well, well,' he replied. 'I have been coming to this church for many years, sitting in this place week after week, without my hat and in all that time, nobody has spoken to me. When I do something wrong, you speak to me!'

Many of us will have had similar experiences of arriving at a church and feeling as though we had entered a private party. Quite often, people don't mean to be unwelcoming – they might be reserved or preoccupied with their own problems. But if you're a parent who has endured a difficult hour or two preparing for church, the last thing you need is a cool or even lukewarm reception.

I was conscious of this as I set out to visit the five different churches in my neighbourhood. On a cold, crisp

February morning, I arrived at St Andrew's Methodist Church. I tried to imagine myself with one or two small children, struggling up the steps and into the church. After taking the decision to attend a morning service, how would I be welcomed by the community? How would I cope with a pram and a toddler? If a church really wants to welcome parents with their babies and children, these are important considerations.

At St Andrew's I received a great welcome. Two members of the church community stood at the door and welcomed all those who arrived. On the morning I visited, a young woman arrived, for the first time, with a child of three and a small baby. 'I want my little girl to go to Sunday school,' she said. She was helped into the church and given advice about the Sunday school and the crèche. When I spoke to her later I asked if she would return. 'Oh yes,' she replied, enthusiastically. 'I really do feel at home here.' (Several months later she was a committed member of the church community.)

Welcoming, for me, means more than kind faces at the door. If I invited my friends to my home and welcomed them with a cheery smile and kept them shivering in the dark and didn't entertain them, I wouldn't expect them to return. The warmth of the welcome needs to extend to the actual physical warmth, too. At St Andrew's great efforts have been made, in recent years, to improve the warmth of the building. About a third of the church has been partitioned off for use as a welcoming and meeting area. The remaining two-thirds is the main body of the church. It is carpeted and warm. I felt comfortable and very much at home there.

At the end of the service, I was greatly impressed with the friendly and welcoming attitude to children. This was evident in the way the congregation greeted many of them as they weaved in and out of people drinking coffee and chatting. Often the antics of the little ones brought smiles and amusement to the faces of the older generation.

At Holy Apostles, the local Anglican church, I received a very positive reply to my inquiries. In a way, the welcome started even before I had set foot in the church. In response to the question, on my initial questionnaire, 'How are parents and small children encouraged to attend your church?' the minister replied:

'It is our intention to present the main church as a welcoming and happy place. The congregation are taught that children are as important as adults and that all church members are responsible for the Christian upbringing of children in our midst. Those who lead worship here must be able to relate to children and babies. In this way we hope that folk with children will keep coming back because they are not regarded as intruders.'

Despite those positive words, I found it daunting to walk into a strange church – it can be even harder if you have one, two or a few children in tow. As soon as I walked into Holy Apostles I received a great welcome. The welcomer's eyes lit up and she shook my hand. 'You're very welcome! Are you new to the area?' she said.

There was a genuine feeling of physical warmth as I walked into the church that morning. Once again, it was a cold morning so the radiators were on full blast and there was a bustling, joyful atmosphere in church with plenty of colourful banners. They provided a stimulating contrast to the high brick walls.

Over the sanctuary was a beautiful stained-glass window and the red-brick interior added to the warmth. Like St Andrew's, Holy Apostles have altered their building to make it more of a focus for the community. About a third of the pews have been removed and there are book stalls and information stands for parishioners. This area is also used after the service for serving tea and coffee.

At Holy Apostles I was told by several people that I had not chosen the right morning to attend. This was something which was said in quite a few churches. However, a parent who wants to take a child to church for the first time, indeed anyone who ventures into a new community alone, chooses a moment that is right in *their* lives – so every Sunday should be right for a new member.

For a parent on the first Sunday, as long as the warmth and the welcome are there, everything else will follow. You can have the most brilliantly run crèche and a superb Sunday school, but if a new member is made to feel like an intruder or a stranger, they may not return. Hospitality and welcome are all-important. Christians are specifically called to welcome the stranger.

At the Elim Pentecostal Church, a member handed me the service books and steered me towards the main meeting room. For me, the welcome began as I walked down a street next to the church as I could hear the beautiful music and singing. It was ten minutes before the beginning of the service and the church was almost full. People sang with gusto, their arms raised heavenward. As I searched for a place to sit, people shuffled along and gestured me to join them.

One parent told me how the welcome and committed approach to her children had encouraged her to become a church member:

———

'We used to go to a Baptist church near our home but we were unhappy with many of the things the minister was saying. We prayed about it and decided to try out different churches. This was the first church we tried and we stayed. There seemed to be a genuine interest in us — they asked for the names and ages of our children, then we were told all

*about the activities available for them. I was given a
statement about the church's policy regarding children.
There's a very special ministry to children in this church
and that's why we're here. We are certain about our faith
in Jesus, we want our children to grow up in the
knowledge and love of Jesus.'*

At Hesed House, Leicester Christian Fellowship,
uniformed stewards greet the community and new
members or strangers. Hesed House is a large converted
factory in an industrial area close to the centre of the city.
It is located in the sort of area from which many other
Christian churches are inclined to retreat. Some Christian
writers, like Bob Holman, are alarmed at the numbers of
churches which move away from poor areas.

---

*'The gospel should be for all, but its resources, efforts and
ministers seem concentrated in the suburbs rather than in
the inner cities and even less noticeable on council estates...
The church should concentrate its efforts on those areas
where the gospel is least heard.'*

Bob Holman, *Towards Equality*, pp. 82–83

It is in these areas that the stranger, especially one with
young children needs to be welcomed and welcomed with
great sensitivity. Potential new members don't need to be

crowded or overwhelmed. If they're genuinely testing the water, they don't want to be pushed in. Being too keen and friendly can be as off-putting as ignoring a stranger. A genuine, sincere welcome is needed.

In my own parish, I see new faces from time to time. I try to talk to them, especially if they have young children. Sometimes they return the following week. Quite often they don't. What happens to them? Did they go to another place where they may have received a better welcome? Or did they prefer a different style of worship? I'm sure a similar scene is played out on Sundays in other church communities. The places I visited made me and other new parents feel very welcome and at home. They have responded to the words of Jesus: 'I was a stranger and you made me welcome.'

Lord, when did we see you a stranger?...

When I visited you on a Sunday with three
small, boisterous children and you lifted
my buggy up the steps.
When you smiled at my children and asked
their names.
When my baby was crying and you stroked
her back and touched my arm to reassure
me.

When my older child tried to run out of the
   doors and you gently guided him back to
   where we were sitting.
When you didn't turn around or tut with
   disapproval when my children were noisy
   and restless.
When you offered to help me just when I felt
   as though I had lost control.

Lord, when did we see you a stranger?

A small sign of support, a smile of approval and the touch of acceptance makes a great welcome for parents who are struggling to do the best for their children. Those fellow parishioners who helped us when our children were small babies have become great friends. Their kindness will never be forgotten.

———

"'Lord, when did we see you a stranger and welcome you?"… And the king will answer, "I tell you solemnly, in so far as you did this to one of the least of these brothers of mine, you did it to me."'

Mark 25:38, 40

Five

Provision for the Child

When my oldest child was a small baby he was 'very good' at church. That's what many parishioners told me. 'Isn't he good,' they cooed, 'he doesn't make a murmur.' It had nothing to do with goodness, much more to do with good timing and luck. I would feed him, discreetly, before the service started and so, naturally, he'd go to sleep.

My 'luck' ran out when he was about nine months old. He wouldn't sleep, he shouted, screamed, cried and as soon as he could move, he noisily started to explore his surroundings. I decided to take him to the crèche. The first week I stayed with him, the second week I left him. He was considerably distressed at his abandonment; so were the helpers.

Thereafter I decided to stay with him and I watched as he moved away from me, always comforted by my presence. After a few weeks of this I began to feel uneasy about being in a crèche and merely playing with my child while a few metres away the word of God was being proclaimed, out of my earshot.

So it is that I have very mixed feelings about crèches for Sunday services. Despite this, I was very impressed with the crèches I did visit, particularly on cold, wintry mornings. Their care and commitment were a great support and witness to many tired parents.

The crèche at St Andrew's has been in existence for almost eight years. The numbers of children fluctuate from week to week – sometimes there may be only one, other weeks six or seven. On the week I attended there were four children between the ages of one and three years. If there's a Christening in the main service, there's often an influx of children.

Each volunteer works about once every four weeks so the children see different helpers each Sunday. 'Otherwise we would never be able to take part in a Sunday morning service.' The crèche was clean, warm and very well equipped. A tape of nursery rhymes filled the room with a relaxing atmosphere as we talked. One of the helpers read stories constantly to the children who obviously felt at home in the crèche. As the children approach their third birthday, these stories are linked more to the Bible and to church teaching but this only happens if the children have been coming regularly and are well known to the helpers.

Despite the good facilities at St Andrew's, it seemed that

the crèche was under-used. The crèche co-ordinator explained why she felt this was so: 'Some people come for a few weeks and then they just stop coming.' Why? 'I'm not sure, really. I don't think it's because they dislike the service, I think it's because other things take precedence. There's Sunday shopping, for instance… and then if you get out of the habit of going to church, it's hard to get back. If you've missed a few Sundays, you almost feel as though people will want to know why you haven't been here…'

But for the parents who were there, the crèche at St Andrew's was of vital importance:

———

'A lot of women attending are married to men who would have no interest in attending themselves and may resent Sunday morning baby-sitting — so from this point of view, the childcare is essential.'

For single parents or those whose partners don't attend church, a crèche provides great support.

Hesed House, Leicester Christian Fellowship, placed childcare provision right at the forefront of its facilities. In 1995 Hesed House won a 'Gold Award' for its services and facilities for children. The certificate is framed and displayed proudly close to the entrance. It was easy to see why.

The crèche for babies from birth to eighteen months was situated close to the front of the complex. There are normally about ten babies present although parents wander in and out responding to the needs of their children, where necessary. Four helpers set up the room with cots, soft play mats, changing equipment and baby toys.

As in many churches, the helpers work on a rota basis and take their turn in the crèche once a month. 'Most of the babies sleep,' a crèche helper told me, 'but if they're awake we play with them and cuddle them. If the children become distressed, we send for their parents.' Parents of very small children are asked to sit in a specific area of the meeting hall so that a steward would be able to locate them easily.

As soon as the children can walk, or when they're eighteen months old, they transfer to the next group, which meets in a larger room. In this group there is time for playing with toys, a Bible story, some simple songs, a drink and a biscuit and more free play. The three- and four-year-olds have a much more structured morning. They have a music and movement session, a story, games, craft activities and free play on some of the bigger pieces of equipment.

Parents and helpers felt that if the children are made to feel welcome and if they are kept busy, they will be happy and will be settled. On the morning I visited, there was a peaceful atmosphere and a good buzz around the young children's activities.

Hesed House appears to have made a conscious decision to welcome the children. The crèche and rooms for the small children are not hidden away at the back of the building. Children are not seen as a noisy problem, as I feel they are in some places of worship. They are cared for in a warm, loving, *Christian* environment. Some parents expressed this in their questionnaire responses:

———

'The childcare is excellent here. My children learn about why we come here every week. It's a relief to know they are being looked after by like-minded people.'

———

'I am really happy with the facilities and resources, the helpers and the involvement expected of me in helping.'

I was greatly impressed by the depth of commitment shown by crèche and Sunday school helpers. At Elim Pentecostal Church, the crèche co-ordinator told me: 'When I come to church on a Sunday, I come to serve. I don't expect anything out of the main worship in church. I am here, merely to serve.' On that morning, such service and commitment were reflected in the welcome and the warmth of the crèche.

There was no doubt that parents felt very relaxed and comfortable about leaving their children in the crèche. The existence of such a facility encouraged parents to come to church, knowing that they would be supported with the care of their children, for at least one morning a week.

The crèche at Elim Pentecostal Church is held in a small room partitioned off the main hall. It is a purpose-converted room with lots of toys, books and baby changing facilities. There is also a small, quiet, warm room at the back of the main church where mothers can breast-feed their babies.

Parents are encouraged to stay with their children if they're fractious or frightened. The morning I visited there were three generations in the crèche: grandmother, daughter and two delightful granddaughters – twins. From the helpers and the parents I heard some interesting stories. First of all, the distance people travel to belong to this church community.

———

'I live seven miles away and many other members live further but there's something about this community – it's so welcoming and has such a positive attitude to children.'

At Holy Apostles, the crèche is held in the vestry at the side of the sanctuary. The room has been carpeted, decorated and furnished so that it resembles somebody's lounge, rather than an impersonal room in church. Parents are encouraged to bring their children to the crèche before the start of the service or during the service if they are crying or restless. The crèche is well equipped with toys and books donated by parishioners. A number of young volunteers take it in turns to care for the children.

Holy Apostles' crèche had been established for a number of years but the arrival of a new vicar, with young children, had helped. One parishioner commented, 'He seems to be more in tune with what children need.' Helpers are encouraged to alternate between the crèche and the Sunday school so that they really get to know the children.

As the children played and a story was read to anyone willing to listen, the service was relayed into the vestry by a speaker. That was useful for parents or carers who were forced to retreat to the crèche and the children seemed to enjoy the hymns they heard. Hearing the service alongside the children, I felt as though there was some connection to the main purpose of being at church on Sunday mornings.

Crèches are not provided in all places of worship. Some places do not feel that they are necessary. At St Theresa's Roman Catholic Church, quite a few families are drawn from neighbouring parishes because they are so impressed with the facilities for young children. Even though there's no crèche – 'Nobody has ever asked for one,' says the

Parish Priest – young children are obviously very welcome here. Indeed, there seems to be little need for a crèche. The noise and bustle of the service seem to be perfectly natural. One parent expressed how she felt about this:

———

'At our other parish, we felt so conscious of the noise of our offspring that we stopped going. A friend told us that this parish was full of noisy children so that one child extra wouldn't be noticed!'

I saw quite a few impressive crèches when I visited churches, all run by dedicated and committed Christians. And yet, although many churches and parents see a crèche as a vital part of the community, I am unsure about their presence and about their function. Is it to keep our church services quiet and our children out of the way? I have mixed feelings. Crèches can be like children's menus in a restaurant – chicken nuggets, burgers and sausages. Are they on the menu to nourish our children or to keep them quiet? Do we present our children with a similar menu in church? Do our churches nurture and develop spirituality in our small children when they are placed in a crèche?

Parents do need time and space to develop their own spirituality and a crèche can help with this. However, I feel that there is a season of parenting and part of that season is developing spirituality with and through our children, not apart from them. A child's screaming and shouting are as much a part of God's creation as the beautiful music prepared by a committed church choir. It is a form of communication – a crying out. When they are placed in a crèche, is it really for the good of children or for the sake of other worshippers whose children have passed beyond this stage?

'There is a season for everything, a time for every occupation under heaven…'

Ecclesiastes 3:1

The season for peace and reflection in my life will return soon enough and I will then probably hanker after the season of noise and bustle. For now, I want to be with my children as they discover the wonder and mystery of God. This is the present season of my life.

But we're all different and crèches do help to encourage parents to develop their faith and, through them, the faith of their children.

Six

Liturgy and Worship

Once I started visiting churches on Sunday, people started suggesting places to me. 'Have you ever been to…?' Even though my main purpose was to look at children's provision, there seems to be a belief that if a place is welcoming, friendly and has good liturgy then the childcare provision will be good. The reality is that many people view worship from an adult perspective and assume that because they find it fulfilling and meaningful, then children will too.

Theologians who study the development of faith and spirituality in children point to the need for spectacle, sound and smell in children's worship. The morning I visited Holy Apostles, there was no Sunday school so the children were in the main service. There was a great deal of joyous singing and that's something which all children enjoy. One child spent most of the service watching the drummer in the church band. The child swayed in time to the music and imitated the drummer's every action.

At other times, children sense the tranquillity of a quiet moment and fill it with a noise which they know will echo around the church. Such a noise brings great delight to a child.

St Theresa's has a slightly different approach to child-care provision. All the children begin the service with their parents and families in the main body of the church. After the opening greeting, the priest invites them to the front of the church where they are encouraged to genuflect before leaving for the Liturgy Group with their leaders. A parent expressed how she felt about this. 'Father John knows each one of these children by name. That, in my opinion, is a great strength. They are seen as important people in the church. Right at the beginning of the service he sets the tone by encouraging the rest of the congregation to pray for the children as they go to their own liturgy.'

———

'I have called you by your name, you are mine.'
Isaiah 43:1

The children moved to a large meeting hall next to the church. Eighteen volunteers, working in four teams, take it in turn to lead the children's liturgy. Each team helps with the children's liturgy once every six weeks. There was great enthusiasm amongst the adult helpers – possibly a result of the work being evenly distributed.

Many of the parishioners love the children's Mass on the first Sunday of the month. The children are involved in the preparation and are encouraged to read out the prayers. One parishioner commented about this: 'The children say many of the prayers and it's lovely to hear how they express themselves so innocently. Like, 'Jesus, I'm sorry for fighting with my brother.' It's a shame adults can't be so brave and open.'

Parents are encouraged to bring their children to the Liturgy Group as soon as they are old enough to sit still and listen to stories, which was what they did on this particular morning. They listened to a simplified extract from St Luke's Gospel:

> Jesus says to his friends,
> 'You must be like your father in heaven,
> full of pity and mercy.
> Never judge anyone.
> Never condemn anyone.
> Always forgive everyone.'

The children later moved to tables for a craft activity or, like the morning I visited, drawing and colouring. The theme for the children's work was, 'Do for others what you want them to do for you.'

The children worked from a worksheet published by

Redemptorist Publications which focused on the gospel reading of the day. They were also encouraged to draw pictures of what they would be willing to share with others during the week ahead. The adult volunteers moved from table to table, giving the children ideas, support, and generally encouraging them.

When the Liturgy of the Word (the readings and homily) had finished, the children returned to the main service. They were greeted by Father John with respect and reverence – their work became an offering and was placed around the altar. The children remained with their families for the rest of the service, walking up to the sanctuary with them at Communion time. As their parents received the Eucharist, they were given a blessing.

The little touches sometimes transform a whole scene for a newcomer to a church. During a part of the service when the priest prays for the people of the parish, he mentioned the youngest member: 'I want you to remember, in a special way, Katie Ann, who was born yesterday. You know her parents.' He named them and he pointed to the place in church where they usually sat. 'That's where they would be with their other children…' The whole parish was informed of the birth. This reinforced the idea of a parish community being like an extended family.

This is a spacious church, built within the last twenty

years. It is a family and child-friendly place. There is space for restless children to wander and indeed, they are acknowledged by the priest if they stray onto the sanctuary. The relaxed atmosphere possibly encourages parents with young children to attend this church – there were certainly many there that morning.

Children were a vibrant and noisy presence in the church. Yet, despite the noise and the bustle, the fidgeting, the crying and the wandering about, there was a prayerful and reverential atmosphere. The tone was set by the respect of the priest towards the whole community, but the children in particular. Some of the parents expressed this in their questionnaire responses:

'I have always been made to feel welcome at this church and children are made to feel a part of it.'

'I find the church atmosphere and the other worshippers friendly and welcoming.'

'I think there are a lot of people working hard to make this parish a real community.'

This indeed, is a child-friendly church. There is a great feeling of support and encouragement for the parents of young children which helps the parents to relax and actually makes children calmer and more peaceful. Children's senses were inspired with the candles, flowers, incense and music. It seemed to me that children were taken seriously in this community. A separate liturgy certainly helped them to understand the main service.

There are some who feel that such separate liturgies are unnecessary and superfluous. When I hear Christians say, 'I don't believe there should be a separate liturgy for children,' I am curious. In most areas of life we simplify written and spoken language so that our children might fully understand what is being communicated. We ensure that any tasks they are given to do are within their capability. Why should this not apply to liturgy and worship?

As a parent, I find it difficult when the sermon is long and academic because my children like to listen to stories told in language that they can understand. I also find it difficult when there's little movement or drama in a service or, heaven forbid, no music. On many Sundays, it is the music which hauls my children back when it feels as though they're on another planet.

A child-friendly liturgy takes preparation and effort. It's a people-friendly liturgy which acknowledges the fact that a real congregation has few theologians and historians but many people who love to listen to good stories. That's what I seek for my children: the words and stories of the Bible spoken clearly and concisely. When my children are spoken to as real people, when they are listened to and when they are involved – then I know the liturgy has real meaning for them.

Seven

Bible Teaching

At a surprisingly early age, children begin to ask very interesting questions and once these questions about faith and spirituality start, they are quite difficult to deal with and they don't go away. It helps to have someone else on your side in the development of faith and spirituality. I found an ally in my child's teacher. One evening, trying to discover what my son had done at school, I asked him, 'Did you have any stories at school today?'

'We had a bit out of the Bible,' he replied.

'Which bit?'

'The bit about Jesus,' he said with a tone of finality, almost as if to say, 'Don't ask me any more.'

Jesus was given more credibility in the eyes of my son because he also heard about him from a teacher – it wasn't just a story, he became more real. I think the same happens when children learn about the Bible at Sunday school

The dedication and commitment of Sunday school

teachers cannot be lost on children. Every Sunday school I visited was a model of a professional, well-run organization with children praying, listening, speaking, singing and playing. There is certainly much for parents to be hopeful about and it helps to know that the little ones are being cared for by Christian leaders who place the children's welfare at the centre of everything.

When I visited Elim Pentecostal Church I loved the way the pastor encouraged the congregation to pray for the children as they left the main hall on their way to the Sunday school. For me, there was a powerful message – Sunday school was not seen as a means of keeping children out of the way while the adults got on with the real business of praying. No, the Sunday school was an important part of the church's activities.

When they are three years old, the children at Elim Pentecostal Church start at the Sunday school, which is held in the church hall. All the children start off in a group in the centre of the hall where they have a song, a story and a prayer together. Then they go into their age-group class where they enjoy a drink and a biscuit before they begin the more serious work.

———

'We must give time and effort to cater in the best possible way for children the Lord gives us. It is vital that we have the right people in leadership of the [Sunday] school and a

*staff who are keen and aware of the responsibilities to teach
the lambs of the flock.'*

Extract from the Elim Pentecostal Church Handbook

There were ten children in the three-to-four-plus group.
They listened quietly to the story, *Jesus and his Friends Go
Fishing*, one of a series of books published by Candle Book
Publishers. (Along with this book there are photocopiable
resources which enable the children to do a variety of craft
activities.) As the children worked on their fishing boat
pictures, they were greatly encouraged by their Sunday
school teachers. There was a lively, caring atmosphere in
the hall.

———

*'The influence of the Sunday school has been felt in the
lives of millions. Its fruits are beyond human reckoning.'*

Extract from Elim Pentecostal Church Handbook

The parents at Elim Pentecostal Church spoke of their
gratitude to the Sunday school teachers for all the help they
were given.

———

*'There are some dedicated members of church who do a lot
to make my church child-friendly. There's a wonderful
Sunday school, parties, outings, games for the children and
a summer school for a week in the summer.'*

'We attend this church because we know that the children enjoy coming and that they receive sound Bible teaching.'

———

'A Sunday school that is operated with vision and vigour and gospel clarity, achieves great things. Like no other agency, they enable us to reach a large part of the rising generation and to bring children and teenagers to Christ.'

Extract from Elim Pentecostal Church Handbook

Every Sunday morning, this church is packed and the crèche and the Sunday school are full of energetic children. The service lasts for about two hours so the members of this community make a considerable commitment each week. Apart from their Sunday service, there are also the many activities during the week. Such commitment to children is inspiring and encouraging.

Hesed House, Leicester Christian Fellowship has many well-furnished and well-equipped rooms at its disposal for teaching the children. They also have many adults who know a great deal about children's likes and dislikes. Here, the three- and four-year-olds occasionally do work from the SALT programme (Sharing and Learning Together, published by Scripture Union); at other times they use materials developed by the helpers.

Although there is an emphasis on Bible stories, there's also a good range of children's literature available. Jane, the helper with this group, explained, 'We need a good range of activities for this age group. They won't settle on one thing for any length of time. We want them to come to an understanding of Jesus in their life, through all the many activities we do here. It doesn't necessarily have to be a Bible story – Jesus is present in other stories.' Many resources are used to provide the best for these children. Helpers often consult the Pre-School Learning Alliance for ideas and advice.

The Sunday school for the three- to five-year-olds at St Andrew's is held in a room at the back of church. There were eight children listening to a story which was based on Psalm 104:

> I bless the Lord: O my Lord God,
>   how great you are!
> You are robed with honour and with majesty
>   and light!
> You stretched out the starry curtain
>   of the heavens,
> and hollowed out the surface of the earth to
>   form the seas.
> You bound the world together so that it would
>   never fall apart.
> You clothed the earth with floods of water
>   covering up the mountains.

You spoke and at the sound of your voice
    the water collected
    into its vast ocean beds...
I will sing to the Lord as long as I live.

After reading the psalm, the teacher involved the children in a dramatic retelling of the story in which they were all given different parts to play. When the children moved to the tables for their second practical activity, which involved drawing and colouring-in, there was a good deal of praise and encouragement from the Sunday school teacher.

There was a great effort, on the part of the community at St Andrew's, to make Scripture relevant to the younger members of the parish. They used stories and practical activities with plenty of interaction. The children were focused on their work and beginning to see the relevance of church and community in their lives. Again, the teacher was using the SALT programme for ages three to four-plus.

———

'You are invited to share in Scripture Union's vision of enabling people of all ages to discover what God is saying through the Bible – not only in separate age groups, but together too. SALT enables your church to learn about the same topics at the same time. Younger children learn in

straightforward ways, using play activities, stories, games and other exciting methods.'

SALT, April–June 1998, Scripture Union

As soon as children start listening to stories and talking about characters in those stories, then they are ready for the Bible. The heroes and heroines of both the Old and the New Testaments have a lot to say, even to the very small children of today. Children want to listen and to learn and it's good that so many church communities have such committed Sunday school teachers to tell those stories. Back in the main church, the community prays for the nurturing of that precious seed of faith, in the Christians of tomorrow.

Eight

Support for Parents

Parents, like teachers and social workers, are often the focus of public criticism. Whatever ails society, parents tend to be held responsible. 'I blame the parents,' older people say, and it's hard, when you're struggling with difficult children, to think of an appropriate response.

Many churches recognize the stress and loneliness involved in parenting and they have responded to a need for meeting places and support for mothers and fathers. In my own neighbourhood, there are activities every day of the week for parents and toddlers, if they wish to attend.

If you're a single parent with small children, perhaps living in a cramped space on a restricted budget, it can be very hard to meet up with other parents, especially in the winter months. There are many play zones and fun factories available for small children but they are costly and generally on out-of-town estates, so requiring personal transport.

Pram Clubs and toddler groups are mainly to be found in church halls. There's a Mums and Tots group on a Tuesday at Elim Pentecostal Church Hall. This is run by members of the church and they see it as a service to the whole community, to support parents and carers. One or two parents of children have become members of the church as a result of belonging to the Mums and Tots group. However, the main purpose of such a group is not to evangelize but to support.

Mary, the leader of the Mums and Tots, said that the helpers use the opportunities for sharing their faith: 'For example, sometimes we read bible stories at storytime, and all parents and carers are invited to family services, especially at Christmas and Easter. As a result of this, some parents have become members of the church.'

Elim Pentecostal also organizes many other activities for small children. There's a summer Bible Club, held for one week during the holidays; a rainbow party on 31 October as an alternative to Hallowe'en celebrations and parties at Christmas and Easter. All local children, as well as children of members, are invited to these events and yes, some of them start coming to church on a Sunday. And they often bring their parents with them.

Recognizing the need for affordable meeting places at weekends, the Elim Pentecostal Church runs a coffee bar on Saturday mornings. Quite often on a rainy Saturday, young families are to be found there. I'm sure the main purpose of such an event is to evangelize and what better way to do this than giving both support and hospitality to those who need it.

St Andrew's also has a weekly Pram Club which is supported by the church minister and many of the church community. Older members of the church help with the preparation of refreshments and listening to parents who may be under great stress. This Pram Club, like many others, also has informal support networks which respond to particular needs. A group of mothers meet regularly and pray specifically for their children. One mother at the group saw the need for prayer as a means of support after listening to the problems of many other mothers.

'One or two of us were really desperate for support with our children and somebody told me about this organization called "Mothers' Prayers" set up by two women in Kent. We started praying together after the Friday group and then we asked others to join us. As we pray about the particular stresses affecting our home, quite often we're able to support one another, outside of this forum. That's how I feel our prayers are answered.'

If you belong to a church or community which is a long way from your home, there are ways of meeting during the week to provide mutual support. At Hesed House the members of the community are drawn from many areas of the city. So, I wondered, how are families, particularly families in difficulties, supported from Monday to Saturday?

———

'It is through the smaller house groups which meet during the week. People know each other well and it is in this setting that any support is provided. They meet the needs of those in difficulty through the smaller groups. They try to involve the children as much as possible so there are fun activities in the house groups, during the school holidays. The aim of these groups is to make church fun and friendly and welcoming so that the children see Christianity as fun.'

At Holy Apostles Church I spoke to a parent helping with the crèche. A child in the crèche began to cry. 'He's just had a baby brother,' she said, 'and he's finding life difficult because he wants more attention.' He was about eighteen months old. She cuddled him and settled down to play with him. Later we talked about the support she had received from the community during the difficult moments in her own life, as a single parent of teenage boys and as a foster mother to many different children. The love and support she had received were, in turn, being passed on to others during the stressful times in their lives.

When I was contacting ministers in local churches I asked for details of how parents were supported by the church community. Most replies gave a list of official church organizations. But beyond those organizations there is a great deal happening and I think many ministers would be surprised to see the network of support which reaches out from the groups listed in Parish Yearbooks.

It reminds me of the way climbing plants attach themselves to a frame or trellis. It is difficult to see how they manage to defy gravity and climb so well. The suckers or tendrils are often hidden. I feel it is like this in many parish communities. The support network, which many don't see, extends far beyond the walls of the church and quite often touches those who otherwise would have nothing to do with a church society.

In my own experience, fellow Christian mothers have supported me through some of the difficult days and nights of parenthood. Though I may sometimes become frustrated with the institutionalized church, I know that it is only through being there and getting to know these people that I have experienced such great goodness. Being with other mothers and fathers who share my vision reinforces my own personal beliefs and helps with the stressful task of Christian parenting.

There's another reason for choosing a community faith for our children. It helps us, as parents, more than we will ever know. It's more than friendship, it's an acknowledgment of our own weaknesses – it is letting go and allowing God, through his instruments on earth, to support us.

———

'When I am weak, then I am strong.'

2 Corinthians 12:10

Nine

Churches and Children

As I visited these few churches I was greatly inspired and encouraged. I witnessed great service and commitment to children and their parents and I saw a very deep faith and love for the gospel. I was profoundly touched by the humanity and goodness of those running facilities for children.

If you, as a parent, are considering joining a parish or church community, there are many ways to start. Talk to others; ask where they worship, and talk about the facilities and resources for babies and children – not just on Sundays but during the rest of the week, too.

Visit the churches in your local area. Take your babies and children and then ask yourself these questions: Where did I receive the best welcome? Where did I feel most at home? Where did I feel that I belonged? Where were my children treated as important and valuable members of the community? Where did I experience the words of Jesus put into practice? 'Suffer little children to come unto me, for theirs is the kingdom of heaven.'

To those parents or church members who are dissatisfied with childcare provision in their churches, I would say – take time out to visit other churches where you know the provision is good. It will help your church community and you, as a person. Then, with a group of like-minded parents, talk to the minister and try to improve the childcare facilities in your own community.

For anyone wanting to set up some form of childcare provision in a church for the main Sunday service, I would offer these words of advice:

1. Involve parents in the planning and running of the crèche. Encourage young helpers but don't rely on them totally. They may not be as committed or inspired as parents and carers – nor should they be. They have different priorities in life.

2. Share the load. The more parents who are involved, the lighter the load and the greater the chance of success. Don't leave all the work to one or two dedicated people.

3. Refer to secular agencies for advice and support. Try contacting the Pre-School Learning Alliance and local childcare information services. Be aware of legislation on

the care of children. Your church minister can help with this.

4. Choose your resources carefully. Toys are important but it helps to be aware that children as young as nine months will listen to simple stories and enjoy singing simple songs. Respond to the needs of the children in the church situation and support parents as they strive to develop a sense of the divine in their children.

5. Having said all that, a good welcome and a positive attitude are more important than expensive resources. One parent, at a church where there was a good crèche, said that she still felt 'unwelcome' by the older members of the community.

6. Encourage your minister and other church leaders to adopt a more child-friendly tone within your parish community.

7. If you are a member of a Pram Club or toddler group, invite parents who show an interest in faith to visit the church. Many parents start attending church because they were invited. It is important for people to know that church communities are open for everyone – they are not exclusive clubs.

8. Make particular use of the church's big festivals – Christmas, Easter, Pentecost – to show parents what's on offer in the church. Mothering Sunday is another important day in many churches and mothers like to be acknowledged for all their efforts. Special invitations will help here.

One of the highlights of my spiritual life was a church service I attended in rural Kenya. The service lasted for well over two hours but it seemed like the shortest I have ever experienced. The music and dancing lifted the spirits continuously. Children sat with their parents or right at the front of church with the choir – they were given homemade instruments and encouraged to play them throughout the service. There was a little wandering about, by the adults as well as the children, but nobody minded. Everyone had to process to the front of the church to make their weekly offering and it was good to see people really involved and not as detached as some church-goers can be.

The church, built of corrugated iron, was full to bursting and there were lots of pre-school children. Yet there was no problem with noise or movement. There was no crèche, the children went to Sunday school in an adjoining building at the age of six. Yes, there were crying, noisy babies but... that's what babies and children do –

they cry, they're noisy. In that church, on that day, children were loved and accepted as they were.

My feelings about the church service in Kenya are reinforced by the words of a missionary working in a refugee camp in the same country:

———

'These people who are always sick, never well-fed, living in mud huts without water, prey to every whim of the police, far from their countries, facing uncertain futures, nevertheless thank God for the graces they have received. They are so joy-filled it is impossible not to be caught up in it – unmerited grace.'

Quoted in Kathy Coffey, *Experiencing God With Your Children*, p. 87

In our own country many churches have responded to the calls within their community for better childcare during services. It can be helpful for parents of babies if there's a crèche or quiet room apart from the main body of the church. They feel under less pressure to keep their baby quiet. However, it's good to hear babies and children making a contribution to the service. It's important to hear crying, chattering, shouting infants. There aren't enough babies crying or gurgling in our churches, we need lots more. As a member of Hesed House said, 'These are the church of tomorrow. They need very careful nurturing.'

People who welcome visitors as they arrive at church

play an important role, especially when parents need support with their small children. My lasting impression of all the places I visited is not the ministers, nor the preaching, nor the singing. It is the welcome. Every church I attended had a welcomer who made me, a stranger, feel as though I belonged there. 'I was a stranger and you made me welcome' (Matthew 25:35).

So, if you're thinking about a community faith for your child, look in the telephone directory, ask around, investigate and search. The church isn't complete without you.

Ten

The Big Question

'Church attendances are falling,' the media report, often with a sense of glee. Yet the churches I visited were full. Not only that, they were also vibrant and alive. So the big question is this: why do people go to church on Sundays? On the questionnaire I gave to parents after visiting each church service, I asked: 'Why do you go to church on Sundays?' These are some of the responses I received.

'Mainly to worship. The atmosphere is a very friendly one. You never feel alone here. I want my children to learn and understand the church.'

'To educate the children in the Bible and encourage them to become more informed people.'

'To worship God with friends and with our second family — the church.'

144

'To give my children the opportunity to form their own opinions on religion. It keeps me in touch with others and gives me a pause for thought.'

———

'The Sunday school needs me and I feel it is important for children to be taught about God's world in an enjoyable way.'

———

'I come to church on Sunday because my child attends Sunday school, but most importantly I believe in God and whenever I'm there I feel a calmness about me and it makes me feel so good about myself and so close to God himself.'

———

'To worship God – to thank him for all his many blessings and to get sustenance for the week that lies ahead. I wouldn't want to be anywhere else on a Sunday morning.'

———

'To meet with God.'

———

'We love Jesus – we want to worship him.'

———

'Because I feel I can worship God in the way I am most comfortable and I know I will get good biblical teaching. I get a lot from fellowship with my fellow Christians with whom I have built up friendships. I also feel that my *children can enjoy being in church... they can learn about God in a lively and exciting way.'*

———

'It's time to focus on the spiritual side of life. It's a community. It's a discipline and a way of life for our child.'

———

'To see my maker.'

———

'I was brought up a Christian and have always attended church on a Sunday so I am carrying on the tradition and faith I have learned from my parents.'

———

'To pray as a family and as a reflection time.'

———

'Because on the whole I enjoy it! Sometimes it is stressful bringing the children and trying to make them behave but I want them to have a religious background and something to help guide them. I sometimes feel guilty if I don't attend. It is also good to be part of a community.'

———

'Why do I come to church on Sundays? Firstly because I love the Lord and want to praise him and thank him and there is nowhere else I would rather be than with other Christians. Also, our Lord commands us to be there; we should set aside everything else on a Sunday. I love to hear the preaching and open my Bible once more. I like to see

everyone and feel blessed after attending church, no matter what kind of week I've had.'

———

'I have learned, over the last five years, to pray and ask God to help me through problems, and he does. He is my best friend, he is my peace.'

———

'I want to worship God, although with a young family and both myself and my husband actively involved in the children's work on a Sunday morning, it is very hard. But we feel we want to serve God in this ministry.'

———

'We worship God – to learn from his word, to be encouraged, uplifted. To have fellowship with other believers, to work together to bring more people to know the love of Jesus.'

———

'To worship and praise God and to hear the Word preached. I think this is carried out well, right through to the younger children. My four-year-old always talks about what she has learned and sings most of the day after Sunday school.'

———

'I come because I believe and am committed to regular church attendance. I find it refreshing and uplifting and I would feel very isolated without the teaching and fellowship.'

'Because we love Jesus and enjoy getting together with Christians. We also know that it's part of God's plan for our lives to be part of this local church.'

———

'To show publicly my love for God, to worship and give thanks. To relieve the sometimes stressful and negative experiences of non-Christian friends.'

———

'To worship God and to hear him speak to me in a corporate setting; to be with the family I belong to. I don't believe you can be a Christian without being part of a local body, from which it follows you must meet together – Sundays or whenever.'

It's impressive to read why people attend church and the power of the faith encourages me, as a parent. Some questionnaires gave no response to the big question – it's hard for some to articulate about something so close to their hearts. I am not sure how I would have responded myself because I have always attended church on a Sunday. As a child I went to morning Mass and Evening Devotions and I loved going to both. I loved the music, the candles, the incense, the drama, the getting dressed up in my best clothes and the laughs we had walking to and from church. That was what we did, that was that.

Nowadays, I go because I help with the music and I'm

conscious of my personal commitment to this. I want my children to grow up in the love and knowledge of Jesus and I want them to belong to a Christian community – it is our extended family.

There's another reason, too – it is in the rare, quiet moments of prayerful thought that I experience real peace. It is these precious moments which keep me going during the week. These are the times away from the rushing; away from the expectations and the pressures; away from the stress and the demands. In these gentle pauses I hear the word of God. Quite often, it's a simple phrase:

> This is what Yahweh asks of you, only this,
> that you act justly,
> that you love tenderly,
> that you walk humbly
> with your God.
>
> Micah 6:8

Quite often this text, sung in the hymn written by Mary McGann (in *More Songs of the Spirit*, published by Kevin Mayhew), moves me to tears. This is all the Lord asks of me and I am in awe of the simplicity and purity of that message.

The moment passes but it refreshes and renews me, ready for a week in the church of our home.

Now that's another thing…

Eleven

Celebrate!

One of the most brilliant things about being a parent is that you experience childhood again – through the senses of your own children. Young children are so full of wonder, so devoid of cynicism, sarcasm and irony. When they look into a cage at the zoo and say, 'Isn't Joey a beautiful chimpanzee!' they mean just that. They also soak up so many experiences in such a positive way, reminding us that there is so much about our world that is good.

Another great thing about being a parent is being able to establish a new culture in your own home. It's up to every parent how that culture is shaped and formed and what affects the development of the culture. It is too easy to be influenced by the materialism which is thrust at us every day through advertisements on billboards, in the press and on television. 'If you want to be a good parent, if you want to do the best for your child,' they tell us, 'then you *must* have this.'

Before long our children are also affected by this and we

may sometimes feel as though we're on a treadmill or a hamster wheel which never stops turning because we can never have everything.

If you are searching for something extra for your child and yourself, or if you want your life to be shaped by the gospel teachings of Jesus, first of all remember his words:

———

'Come to me, all you who labour and are overburdened, and I will give you rest. Shoulder my yoke and learn from me, for I am gentle and humble in heart, and you will find rest for your souls.'

Matthew 11:28–30

Our children do not need every toy that is advertised on television; it is not important for them to have designer clothes or the latest model in buggies or high chairs. They need so much more than the world says they must have.

When my children were baptized, we promised to raise them as Christians. We were appointed as the first teachers of our children. (I realize that infant baptism isn't the tradition for everyone, but whatever the tradition we are still called to be teachers of our children.) Now teachers do a great deal more than take a child to church once a week. For us, as the first teachers of our children, that was part of the promise but it certainly wasn't the most important element of our vow.

We try to follow and celebrate the church's year in our home. During Advent we had a little ceremony each evening to encourage our children to prepare for the birth of Christ in a simple, wholesome way. If we don't make a point of acknowledging the spiritual significance of Advent, then it becomes a materialistic dash to pile up consumer goods for the big feast. Such feverish preparation brings disappointment and disenchantment in its wake.

'Come to me all you who labour...' We took a breathing space for a few minutes, with our children, each day during Advent. Christmas was so much sweeter. We lit a candle and opened a window on the Advent Calendar each evening and then we said a simple prayer together: 'Jesus, come into my heart this Advent.' On Christmas day my son asked, 'When are we going to light the candle again and ask Jesus to come into my heart this Advent?' His face fell when I told him that Advent was over. 'Does that mean we can't have the candle any more?' he wanted to know. In four weeks he had grown to love this simple, peaceful ritual.

Having simple rituals during the special seasons of the year helps children to understand the importance of faith in your own home. As the children grow it becomes a focal point and an opportunity for discussion and dialogue.

All the important feasts can be celebrated in a special

way at home. At Christmas it's good to have a crib as well as a Christmas tree. A small ceremony unveiling the crib on Christmas Eve, or placing the child Jesus in the crib on Christmas morning, helps the children to understand the real meaning of the season. In the buying of presents for children, it's good to remember the motto, 'Live simply, so that others might simply live.' We try to keep things simple and avoid too much materialism – especially in the build up to the so-called 'Festive Season'.

Since my children were born, at birthdays we try to celebrate the gift of life that has been given to us. I also think a child's birthday is a chance to celebrate motherhood and fatherhood. As well as presents and parties, it's good to talk to children about the day of their birth – where they were born, the time, the weather and any other details they may want to know. For each child, the day of their birth is very important and we acknowledge the special gift we received on that day.

There are many publications which suggest lots of ideas for celebration and worship at home. Children find it easy to participate if there's something concrete and something for them to do – like blowing out a candle and singing.

We celebrate anything and everything in our home – it helps to punctuate our lives in a positive way, especially when times are hard and life seems to be quite a drudge. Through our celebrations we remember the words of Jesus when he said, 'I have come so that they might have life and have it to the full' (John 10:10). And surely that's what all parents want for their children.

We are the first teachers of our children. They look to us for love, guidance and support. All our words and actions shape their being. Their personalities are formed by the manner in which we speak to them; praise them and encourage them; discipline them; train them; nourish them and play with them.

Paul writes in the Bible, 'Faith comes by hearing' (Romans 10:16–17), and it is through parents that children first hear about God. The church of our homes is, therefore, vitally important for the whole of the church.

Our home is the most important spiritual resource in the life of our children. Yes, we are sustained by the wider church but it is the values they hear and experience at home that matter the most. Jesus said, 'When two or three are gathered together, I am there in their midst.' Well, there are four in our home and we know he's here beside us, carrying us, soothing us, calming us when we feel the disturbed nights, the tantrums and the fights over food are stretching us to breaking point.

He's also here with us in our joyful moments of celebration – our Advent, Christmas, Easter, our holidays, and the days one of us learns to read or masters the art of riding the tricycle.

'Come to me all you who labour…' At the end of a long, hard day, I know he's here. I've seen his face in my children as they cuddle up to me for a bedtime story. I've also seen his face and felt his presence in the many people who have helped me to the end of this book. I hope you, too, will discover his presence in your children, and through your faith and goodness, you will sow the seeds of love.

You have given them life – help them to live it to the full.

Acknowledgments

Thanks to the following for their time and honest responses to my many questions: Amanda Biggs, Michelle Bohill, Father Joseph Carty, Karen Colvin, Father John Daly, Tracey Elliott, Margaret Farrell, Jackie Hopewell, Sarah Hoskin, Kar-li Leung, Erika Parker, Carmel Peacock, Helen Pinney, Clare Pollard, Louise Roadknight, Ruth Souter, Pastor Tonks, Kate Tyler-Geary, D. Watkins.

Thanks to the following church communities:

St Andrew's Methodist Church; Elim Pentecostal Church; Hesed House, Leicester Christian Fellowship; St Peter's Roman Catholic Church; St Theresa's Roman Catholic Church.

Also thanks to my Mum and Maurice, Ruairi and Mairi Frances for their patience and love. Thanks, most especially, to Ian for his great support.

Bibliography

Kathy Coffey, *Experiencing God with Your Children*, Crossroads, 1997.

Bob Holman, *Towards Equality*, SPCK, 1997.

Jill Murphy, *A Quiet Night In*, Candlewick Press, 1998.

Michael and Terri Quinn, *From Pram to Primary School*, Family Caring Trust, 1995. Family Caring Trust can be contacted at 44 Rathfriland Road, Newry, County Down, DT34 1LD, Northern Ireland.